Spiritual Heritage And Cultural Symbols of India

Arise Awake Attain

By

Jhaver P. Shreenivas

JAICO PUBLISHING HOUSE

Mumbai ● Delhi ● Bangalore
Calcutta ● Hyderabad ● Chennai

SPIRITUAL HERITAGE AND CULTURAL
SYMBOLS OF INDIA
ISBN 81-7224-736-2

First Jaico Impression: 1999

Published by:
Ashwin J. Shah
Jaico Publishing House
121, M.G. Road
Mumbai - 400 001.

Printed by:
R.N. Kothari
Sanman & Co.
113, Shivshakti Ind. Estate,
Marol Naka, Andheri (E),
Mumbai - 400 059.

DEDICATION

THIS VOLUME IS DEDICATED TO SCHOLARS OF OCCULT SCIENCES. TOTAL PROCEEDS RECEIVED BY THE AUTHOR FROM THIS SOURCE SHALL BE UTILISED FOR ECOURAGING ADVANCED STUDIES.

JHAVER P. SHREENIWAS

ABOUT THE AUTHOR

Mr. Shreeniwas was born in a pious family at Gwalior on 18th July 1917. In '1937' he joined State Bank at Indore. In '1949' he joined a British firm as Manager at Delhi. During his stay in Delhi he was elected Director of Rotary when there was only one Rotary Club in New Delhi. In 1966 he became General Manager of Hindusthan Sugar Mills Ltd., the largest sugar producing mill in Asia; and in 1968 he was appointed Chief Executive of Shree Digvijaya Cement Co. Ltd. at Bombay.

To be of service to society, he became Secretary of Bal Bharti, an institution established for teacher's training and education from Primary upto Post Graduation; Jt. Secretary of Bhartiya Kala Kendra (Now Sir ShreeRam Kalakendra), Vice president of Gandharva Mahavidyalaya, and Lok Kalyan Samity — an institution established by Hon'ble Sucheta Kriplani; All these institutions enjoy international reputation. LKS is devoted to the service and help of slum dwellers and poorer sections of Delhi. LKS owns one of the finest eye care hospital in India. Thus, despite hectic life he devoted time to be of service and help to the weaker sections of society.

He specialises in Acupressure Therapy blended with yogic exercises and gives FREE treatment to the needy.

This philanthropic experience moved him to read spiritual literature most of which is in Sanskrit or translation thereof in English and other languages, detailing vi

the laudable achievements of Rishis and yogis; but those heights are unattainable by worldly persons, so he contacted enlightened souls to ascertain the metaphysical successes attained by modern Scientists, clairvoyants and Saints. This authentic collection and compilation illuminates a renaissance in spiritual heritage for aspiring minds to persue Spiritual paths of Sublimation and bliss. To realise HIM is the supreme goal of human existence and that He can be realised through many chosen paths. Vedant teaches good of all. Indian Philosophy reveals process of immediate perception and experience rather than abstract scepticism and arguments. Amen!

CONTENTS

viii

PREFACE

"giranch gaurim girisham ganesham gurunch geervāna
gurum grahēsham;
pranamya pitrorapi pādpadma, pravachmi āryan sanskrati
lālityam."

I touch the lotus feet of Gods, Nature, teachers, ancestors
for beatitude of this compilation of Aryan culture.

All civilisations have left behind magnificent symbols
revealing the supreme heights attained and enjoyed by
people living in that era. Distinctive and popular items were
chosen as symbols of culture; On seeing a symbolic item,
a vivid picture of that country and era emerges in mind.
Symbols of sovereignty and power over world's temporal
and spiritual life — emblems of divine and human
sovereignty; a symbol must necessarily suggest more than
what it expresses.

From times immemorial, Indians have always drawn
inspiration from the soil and environment so, all our
cultural symbols are associated with the leaves, fruits,
flowers, birds, animals, reptiles etc. All auspicious
occasions are celebrated with such symbolic items and to
ensure adherence, Rishis associated symbols with the
ceremonies as essential ingredients. Our heritage has a rich
inventory of attractive and inspiring symbols; Every symbol
is pragmatic like a tiny seed which proclaims its potentiality
of becoming a blooming tree. A careful look at the symbols
opens up a vista of knowledge and the success achieved in

humility and dignified living style is the beacon of a progressive civilisation.

"tyāgēnaikē amrutatavmānusha"

Through renunciation alone some have attained immortality. There can be no spiritual strength until an individual renounces worldly materialism. Robots behave like human beings without intelligence whereas even a tiny insect behaves intelligently for self-preservation. Providence has placed human beings highest on the evolutionary scale. Western Scientists, thinkers as well as commoners are undergoing a transformation. The knowledge of basic truths of life will be of use to all persons searching for lasting peace and salvation. Rishis have charmed and delighted foreigners with clairvoyant vision perceiving through the cosmos the minutest, the distant and the hidden mysteries. This volume is an attempt to present the divine principles and attainments of Rishis. Dependence on legends, myths, miracles has been avoided. Rishis were true world leaders and teachers in trigonometry, quadratic equations, grammar, phonetics, science, geomancy and the religion called Dharmā (Duties).

＊＊＊

PRELUDE

durlabham bhārtē janma | Birth in Bharat (India) is rare.

They are lucky who take birth in Bhārat, a land where GODS also crave to be born. Our Vedic civilisation was the product of the efforts of divine incarnations like Shree Rāmchandra, Yogēshwar ShreeKrishna, omniscient Rishis and sages. Rishis have said that all shall attain Moksh (Salvation) through evolution; With Guru Krupā and soul purification efforts one can accelerate liberation so, everyone has to make a start towards this process; Initially one receives emotional inspirations from surroundings and reading; After satisfying the intellectual urges, one can dive deep into spirituality under vibrating guidance of a Siddha Guru who perceives in the desciple's consciousness and his devotion, not his status.

The word civilisation denotes the cumulative spiritual and cultural heritage of a nation or a race in a given era. It reveals the character and conduct of persons and the society of that age. The Westerners had developed by far in materialism. After the visit of Swami Vivekānand, Swāmi Prabupād, Swāmi Muktānand, Shree Pāndurang Shāstri and his Swādhyayee millions a "sanskrati vistāar" — cultural renaissance has taken roots. Thus civilisation and culture are complementary like the skin of mango or the peel of orange. Even the fragrance of these celestial fruits is rich and rejoicing. Similarly, intellectual advancement with revealing the mysteries of nature in universe. The beauty and pervasiveness manifests itself in our code of conduct in life.

Intellectual discussions were common but neither force nor compulsion were the basis of dharma as is reflected in "avibhaktam vibhvāteshū; Unity in diversity. Great Rishis — Balmiki, Vashishtha, Vishwamitra, Gautam, Agastya, Sandilya, Bhardwaj, Ptanjali and others propagated "tatva-samanvayat" — respect for all religions. For all words of wisdom without any trace of bitterness or fundamentalism. Despite numerous religious discourses amongst our multi-ethnic populace, we had a pluralistic society, preaching and advocating development and progress to attain sublime heights in thoughts and actions. Sacred symbols can be seen in religious rites where they transpose their meaning to a metaphysical sense. Rites possess an efficacy of their own and serve as a means to desired ends. To see in symbols the influence it embodies is like looking beyond the letter of any text to discover its spirit. Adherance to its outward form degenerates into superstition. Many holy symbols are unique, without parallel in shape size, quality and virtue. Rishis had converted abstracts into systematic melodious sounds and different colours were ascribed to supreme or debased aspirations and emotions.

Idols or structures are picturesque depiction of the visions of their artists so they have inherent limitations because they are the creation of imperfect human beings; whereas symbols are mostly products of Nature with inherent beauty, fragrance and expressiveness of praise-worthy sentiments. By themselves they do not generate disputes of caste, colour, or creed. They have universal appeal. Generations of research, experimentation and self- experience of beneficial results enjoyed by Rishis proclaim that every symbol has miraculous beneficial potency; with proper usage one can enjoy the blessings but its inverse/perverse use can end up in destruction. Different forms of Gods and Goddesses are not mere imitation of different concepts or thoughts; They are symbols of different virtues and powers. For instance, mythology shows Lord Vishnu sleeping on the cosy bed of Sheshnāg's coils for 4 months, every year. Gitā proclaims that GOD does not rest even for a blink of eyes. As such, the restful picture of Lord Vishnu is symbolic of accurate, precise and perfect creation in all functions; That nothing can go wrong even if GOD goes into deep slumber for months together. Discreet understanding elevates every person in joy. Mathematical explanation of idolic symbols yields sublime appreciation. Rishis had visualised the omnipotence of gods and goddesses in figurative terms. Brahamā is called Chaturānan — 4 headed to represent 4 Vedās; Lord Shiva is called Trinetra, denoting past, present and future periods of universe; 4 hands of Vishnu symbolise round the clock action to propagate/preserve life; or 4 objects of life to be attained by every person Dharma (duty), Arth (prosperity), Kama (sex) and Moksh (Salvation). Shiva also signifies — Trinity Sat-Chit-Anand — Truth, Awareness and Bliss. The primordial energy is personified in Ardh- Nārishwar a deity half-male and half-female; A symbol of unity and harmony because with the omnipotency of Adishakti, Lord Shiva destroys evils. To express this supernatural might, Adishakti assumes many forms and functions with 4 or more hands as demanded by the situation.

Lord Shiva is also depicted as NEEL-Kantha-GOD with blue throat because HE alone agreed to drink the deadly poison obtained from ocean churning. The significance of this depicting is that GOD did not want human beings to become addicts of drugs/poisons/intoxicants; HE retained the deadly poison in HIS throat to reveal that if addictions go to heart, they become deadly; HE does not spit out the poison lest it consumes the universe; To emphasise this aspect Shiva wears growing moon and cooling ganges on HIS head — balanced living.

Curiosity about different forms of Gods & Goddesses has a scientific explanation. Every person is enchanted with a particular charming aspect or concept, so in his ecstasy he starts singing the praise of that form, which in terms of musical notes denotes peculiar waves/vibrations; In Music one can create any shape/form of concerned deity as may be conceived for his cherished desire. Thus, Rishis opened all possible avenues for sublimation in life and living style to depict through cultural symbolism.

gun kriyānusāren kriyatē roop kalpanā!

Idols are conceived in thoughts, then sculptured or cast for impressive reproduction of virtues visualised in the deity. Different colours, armaments, ornaments, decorations, vehicles are used to give depth and meaning, linked with environment, development and progress. Any serious talk about rights is meaningless without concept of responsibility. Human rights were recognised and respected with developmental efforts and ecology for long term sustainability of country's resources; The dictum being — "Every right one has springs only from a duty fulfilled".

Vedant discovers the truths of inner world and synthesizes them with the sciences of the outer world to present a unified vision of total reality, and to impart to human life and character depth of faith and vision alongwith breadth of outlook and sympathy. Vedant does not speak of supernatural revealations. What lies within the sphere of the senses is not the concern of religion because that is the field of the positive sciences.

In recent times in India, it was Vivekanand alone who preached a great message which is not tied to any do's and don'ts. Addressing the nation he said, "In every one of you is the power of GOD; The GOD in the poor desires you to serve HIM." Kazi Nazrul Islam said, "Vivekanand has washed away his stain of separateness of religions and castes by proclaiming from the house-tops the inherent divinity of man." This respect for what is best in man proceeds to deliver man from bondage to the slavish part of himself.

Today, the man finds himself deep in a situation where his past glory is unrecoverable, his present uncertain and his future an interrogation. In human history man had never experienced so much darkness within him in the light of all-round enlightenment out-side of him; So much inner poverty in the context of measureless enrichment without and so much loneliness in the midst of an environing crowd. All these facts indicate that the whole world is in the throes of a spiritual revolution. A Vedic prayer echoed these pangs saying:

Asto ma sadgamaya; Tamso ma jyotirgamaya; Mrtyor ma amrutam gamaya

From the unreal lead me to the Real; From darkness lead me to Light; From death lead me to immortality. India's spiritual heritage has thus become dear to the hearts of all men and women in East & West. The true glory of men &

women is their inborn divine nature — birthless, deathless, pure and holy. The world is seeking for precisely this spiritual growth for man; it is the only means of breaking through the stagnation which, has come on human mind; the only way to creative living and life's fulfilment.

* * *

INVOCATION

"OM Pūrṇamadah Pūrnamidham, Pūrnāt Purnmudachyatē,
Pūrnasya pūrnamādāya, Pūrnmevavāsisyatē. Om shānti,
shānti, shāntih!'

The invisible Braham is the FULL; The visible (world)
too is FULL. From the FULL (Braham) the FULL
(universe) has come. The FULL Braham remains the same,
even after the FULL (universe) has come out of FULL.

This verse is very profound in meaning and significance;
It reveals the grasp, sweep and - scope of WHOLE.
Manifestation, not creation is the word of science today.
Every step we take in life has fulfilment as its goal; the urge
to wholeness as its motive. Man's destiny is to make
possible greater fulfilment and for achievement for human
society.

The achievement of human destiny cannot be left to be
worked out by the evolutionary processes of nature. Shall
we just float with the current of nature and achieve
fulfilment as and when nature achieves it for us? OR shall
we take our destiny from the hands of Nature into our own
hands and achieve it by ourselves. Huxley said, "Man with
his intelligence and imagination, has the capacity to direct
his evolution and quicken its pace in himself and in his
environment".

One curious fact present in the midst of all our joys and
sorrows, difficulties and struggles is that we are journeying

towards progressive freedom; True freedom and bliss through the realisation of our real spiritual nature.

Two kinds of persons are happy and free from tensions either the utter fool or one who has surpassed himself and has become one with GOD. All others are in varying stages of sorrow and tensions. Such persons are happy with the little pleasures they get in the sense-world; such beams of occasional happiness is their mighty relief in worldly chaos. Remember "the boat should be in the water but water should not be in the boat". Today worldliness has overtaken us; we yearn for name and fame as an end in itself; This attitude has retarded our spiritual progress. Remember that to have achieved human birth is also a great thing in the march of evolution. Intense dissatisfaction with the present worldly charms and a keen desire to scale further heights are true marks of moral and spiritual greatness. This realisation can be achieved with a purity of vision and a determined effort to cleanse our thoughts and living styles. Butter is present in milk, but it needs churning to bring it out. So is the truth hidden in sublime experiences.

* * *

AUM

The earliest human beings learnt that the source of life is breath. Analysis revealed that inhaling air generates SH-SH sound while exhaling is associated with HM-HM and enunciated that SOHAM is the keynote of life. Later it was discovered that different sounds could be uttered in combination with different limbs of body — the sound O was gutteral, the Sound 'am' touched palate, and was completed at the lips etc. So he danced with glee and discovered that his body was radiating joy which bellowed and sounded AUM and he believed that AUM encompassed his total existence. His inquisitive mind continued to delve deep into the mysteries of Nature to ascertain the meaning and potency of different sounds/utterances/pronunciations. This made him aware of sounds created by rustling winds, leaves, chirping birds and thundering clouds; Man also observed that different sounds produced specific pattern of waves and vibrations; That sound waves below 30 cycles per second and above 15000 cycles were not clearly audible to human ear. Observing the infinite potencies of the sounds generated in cosmos due to vibratory atomic energies, the Rishis alloted materialising values to every alphabet. This truth is the basic of Coueism and similar systems of psychotherapy:

"aitādhye vākshram Braham, aitādhye vakshram param".

"AUM is Braham; Whoever knows this reality hidden

behind the sound AUM, obtains whatever he desires. Thus nādbrahm became the first symbolic GOD."..... Kathopanishad.

"A kind of waking — Chaitanya, trance — half-asleep, wrote poet Tennyson, "which I have frequently had from boyhood onwards, whenever I have been alone. This has come upon me through repeating my own name to myself, silently, till all at once, as if it were out of the intensity of the consciousness my individuality itself, seemed to dissolve and fade away into boundless being, surest and utterly beyond words — where death was an almost laughable impossibility, as if it were the loss of my individual personality into the true life of myself. It is NO nebulous ecstasy, but a state of transcendental wonder associated with absolute clearness of my mind".

Schlegel, a great Western thinker said, "Even the loftiest philosophy of Europeans, the idealism of reason as set forth by Greek philosophers appears, in comparison with the abundant life and vigour of Oriental idealism, like a feeble Promethean spark against a full flood of Sun light. What distinguishes the VEDĀNT from all other philosophies is that it is a happy blend of religion-cum-philosophy; in India, these two are inseparable".

The potencies of sound and 'VACHĀ' (human speech), were profoundly investigated in India. The 'AUM' sound vibrating throughout COSMOS has three manifestations or virtues; those of creations, preservation and destruction as written in Taittiriya Upnishad. Every time, a person utters any letter or word, he puts into operation, one of these three potencies of AUM. This is the lawful reason behind the exhortation of all the scriptures that man must speak only the truth. The ideal of SATYA (truth) has permeated Hindu society. Marco Polo had written that a holy Brahmin will never utter a lie for any thing on earth. As such Brahmins enjoyed VĀCKHĀ-SIDDHI; and could speak with absolute authority and it always came true to the letter.

Arnold Mathew said, "Mans body battery is not maintained by eatables alone, but by the vibratory cosmic energy — AUM. This invisible power flows into the human body through the gate of Medulla Oblongata but originates in Thalamus — the seventh bodily center located in mid-brain called the SAHASRĀR, the last and ultimate location of Kundalini, above AGYĀ-CHAKRA. The Medulla is the Primary channel for the body's supply of life force, best known as PRĀN or AUM. It is directly connected with man's will-power, concentrated in the SAHASRĀR. Cosmic energy is stored in the brain as the reservoir of infinite potentialities mentioned in VEDĀS as the 1000 petals of the lotus of light. When — the authors of Bible refer to the word 'Amen' or the Holy Ghost, they invariably mean AMEN OR AUM — the invisible life force which divinely upholds all creations.

American Indians are known for having developed sound rituals for rain and wind. Tansen, the great Indian singer in Akbar's court had lit up all the candles in Darbar-Hall by singing DEEPAK-RĀG; and his beloved Tani had quenched the flames which had engulfed Tansen, with Rāg-Megh-Mallahār. The miracles of sound-modern TV and radio are instrumental versions of catching and transmitting sound waves, but they lack the potency of materialising, enjoyed by Rishis. A very suggestive illustration to explain this phenomena is that after turning a stringed instrument to a particular pitch, strike the corresponding note on a piano and you will notice that whenever this particular note on the piano is sounded it creates a corresponding vibration in the stringed instrument even when it may be placed at a distance from the piano.

* * *

PRANAYAM
COSMIC ENERGY CONTROL

Pranayam is normally understood as the science of breath. The correct literal meaning of this Sanskrit word is — Prān=Energy; Āyamā=manifestation or control. Prān is the vital energy in the Universe and all living beings enjoy it throughout their life time. Just as an iron piece becomes a magnet when passed through electricity; similarly universe is vibrating with prān-vāyu and mother nature generously gives it to all those who can draw it upto the full measure of their capacity.

Generally people confuse prān with oxygen and normally they draw in only around 20% of their lung capacity because of ignorance of the science and technique of correct and efficient breathing. A normal person breathes upto fifteen times in a minute, whereas yogis can remain breathless for as long as they choose or decide -- interesting paradox! Our Rishis had learnt and mastered the secret; however modern doctors and scientists are perplexed with the phenomena.

According to ancient Yoga Shastras the prān is classified under five major heads — Prān, Udān, Samān, Apān, and Yyāna; With a happy and harmonious blend these fine classifications are cumulatively denoted by the single word — prān; Its governing body is breath. Rishis Pātanjali has written the magnificent Yoga-Sutra to clearly define and detail the science and control of breath. To understand it

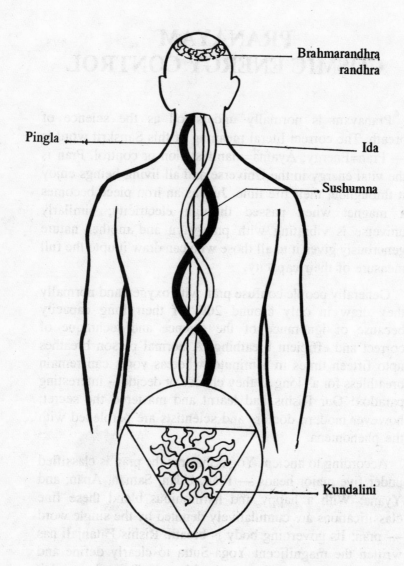

Brahmarandhra randhra

Pingla

Ida

Sushumna

Kundalini

better, one must have a clear knowledge of the nature and functioning of nervous system; basically it is the regulation of inhalation and exhalation of breath combined with retention power.

By regulating the functioning of lungs, one acquires control over the heart and vagus nerves; This is accomplished by controlling the pause between inhalation and exhalation. The autonomic nervous system regulates processes in our body such as secretions by digestive organs, the heart beat etc. but with Prānayāma, voluntary control over autonomic nerves can be largely achieved and modulated. It is for this reason that control of breath constitutes the starting point for controlling the autonomic nervous system; A determined effort holds the key. Detailed knowledge and perseverance is needed to learn all about the finer forces of LIFE instead of rhetoric about intake of oxygen and exhalation of carbon dioxide, because Pran flows throughout the body through thousands of channels called Nādies.

Animals have simple openings or holes through which the air enters their nasal cavity; Only human beings are gifted by Nature with a mysterious and complex nose with two distinct divisions called nostrilles which are divided by a septum.

The distinction between breathing through the right and left nostril was deeply studied by Rishis and they discovered that the flow of air through the right nostril gears the internal organs towards more active physiological processes; Drinking water is a passive kind of intake and this conclusive study gave birth to Swara-Yoga — The process and methodology of uttering/making sound with correct pronunciation/punctuation. Breathing through the right side made a person more active and alert; breathing through the left side produces a quieter, more passive psychological state, so the Rishis considered the side through which the air was flowing in or out to be extremely important for all their activities; This study provided the basis for preparing mentally, emotionally and physiologically for any activity. Thus the functioning and utility of two important nadies was revealed.

Later it was discovered that besides Pinglā (Sun Nādi) which flows through the right nostril, and Ida (Moon-Nādi) flows through left nostril there exists a middle passage which they named as Sushumnā which passes through the junctions of Pingla and Ida nādies, was of prime importance for meditation. All these three major nādies originate at the base of the spine and travel upwards, along the spinal canal and terminate in Sahsrār (Thalamus) corresponding to the ventricular cavity of the physical body.

The junctions of these three nadies, along the spinal canal are called Chatrās or wheels; Just as the spokes of a wheel radiate outward from the hub, so do these three nadies from the Chakras to other parts of body. There are seven principal Chakras as illustrated below, uniting the Sahasrār. Scientists have not yet succeeded in identifying these three basic nādies which are the core of Prānāyama. Yoga anatomy and physiology is very clear and accurate for those who systematically practice and study the science of breath and yoga.

Prānāyam devitalises the Idā and Pinglā, but at the same time it opensup Sushumnā nadi, thus allowing the cosmic energy to flow through this channel freely. The Yogi then

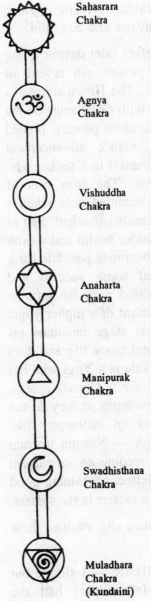

Sahasrara Chakra

Agnya Chakra

Vishuddha Chakra

Anaharta Chakra

Manipurak Chakra

Swadhisthana Chakra

Muladhara Chakra (Kundaini)

experiences great bliss and is freed from the bondage of time, space and causations; He becomes one with GOD and attains freedom from the cycles of birth and death.

Divine feats are required against incurable diseases or insoluble human problems. The masters who have become one with HIM exercise miraculous powers solely for the good of humanity or other living entities. ALL great ones become NOT VIRTUOUS BUT VIRTUE — This is the sole purpose of creation by GOD. Rishis had discovered this energy source pervading in cosmos and developed Pranayama technique called Kundalini to harness it. Those who succeed in arousing the Kundalini acquire the powers of becoming omniscient and omnipotent.

No event, rare or phenomenal is without law or beyond law. Self-realised sages can perform miracles because they understand the subtle laws of Creation; Each one approaches GOD in his own way just as two grains of sand are not alike. Yoga Vidya is a codified system. It has eight phases for self-realisation. They are — Yama, Niyam, Asana, Prānāyam, Pratyāhāra, Dhāranā, Dhyāna and Samādhi.

King JANAK led the life of a perfect saint despite being a good householder. No worldly person can reveal all KARMA -- deeds of previous births. The Hindu scriptures exhort devotees that total mergence with GOD must be the goal. The incidental mastery of miraculous powers, if used for worldly purposes, delay a man's advancement indefinitely; GOD does not reveal himself to a seeker who is satisfied with lesser attainments. The iron bits of KARMA — worldly activities get attracted only when a magnet of personal ego exists and remains attached. Just as worldly wise persons delusively consider health and wealth to be their goal in life, similarly it becomes possible for a devotee, who might have attained some success and spiritual progress, to become infatuated with the gifts or powers which accompany the attainment of a higher yogic stage called SIDDHI. However that stage becomes his downfall until he reverts to a holy and pious life and does penance. The only exception to this rule is a Yogi who has attained and established himself in Infinite Consciousness, his actions and miracles are for benevolence so they do not become , because he then becomes an instrument like ARJUNA to perform the divine wish — Nimitta mātram bhava sabya sāchī — ''Oh Arjuna become an instrument only'' Just as the postman delivers letters containing good or bad news to the addressee, is only a carrier in the system.

Some European and Arab saints have also attained these sublime heights.

Ordinary folk like GORA KUMBHAR — a simple but KARM-YOGI potter of India (Maharashtra) had the courage to tell saint Namdeva that he was immature in YOGA even when Namdeva had established kinship with Yogeshwar SHREEKRISHNA, similar to HIS classmate SUDĀMĀ; Saint Namdeva instantaneously realised his short coming, approached his Guru to lead him on royal path of YOGA and attained salvation.

Bhagwan BUDDHA had evolved a simpler system of Prānāyām, called Vipashyanā which can be persued in daily life by householders and others. The basis of this is balanced concentration and the control of one's breathing system+moun (absolute silence) — the avoidance of avoidable speaking, enabling a person to have a cool mind to think and persue sublimation in all walks of life. This system of Pranayam is taught by Shri S. Goenka at his Ashram located at Igatpuri, in Maharashtra (India).

* * *

SANSKRIT

If the Vedic theory of extremely great antiquity of civilised man on this planet is correct, it becomes possible to explain why the world's most ancient tongue — SANSKRIT is also the most perfect. Sir William Jones, the Founder of Asiatic Society has said, "The Sanskrit language, whatever be the antiquity, Is of a wonderful structure; more perfect than the Greek, more copious than Latin, and more exquisitely refined than either of these two languages". Walter Eugene Clark writes about Rishi Panini: "His grammar is the earliest scientific grammar in the world, the earliest compilation of grammar of any language, and one of the greatest ever written". — The legacy of India; Oxford University Press, 1937.

"It was the discovery of Sanskrit by Western writers, at the end of eighteenth century that revolutionised Western study of languages and grammar, and gave rise to our science of comparative philology, but long before that Panini, who names over 60 predecessors, the sounds represented by the letters of the alphabet had been arranged in an orderly systematic form ..... Indian study of languages was as objective as the dissection of human body by an anatomist". The antiquity of Indian civilisation is a subject which the modern scholars are finding full of ethnological interest. According to he Richas (verses), in Vedas, very clear indications are mentioned that BharatVarsh — India had always been the Home of the Aryans. Nothing in Hindu literature or tradition tends to substantiate the writings of Western historians that early Aryans had invaded India from some other parts of Asia or Europe and settled down here. The internal evidence of Vedas which bears on these ethnological points has been presented in an unusual and very readable volume — Rig Vedic India, by Sjt. AbinashChandra Das of Calcutta U'versity, 1921. Professor Das claims that emigrants from India had settled in various parts of Asia and Europe, spreading Sanskrit and Aryan culture and folk lore. For instance, Lithuanians who do not own any great collection of formal literature of their own, do possess a Sanskrit based tongue which is similar to Sanskrit. Lithuanians can understand scholars who speak in Sanskrit. Philosopher Kant, who did not know Sanskrit at all, was amazed at the scientific structure of Lithuanian language. He maintained that, "It possesses the key which will open all the enigmas, not only of philology but also of history". The modern computer scientists have acclaimed Sanskrit alphabet and figures to be universely adaptable for computers.

True, the Vedas were memorised, but it does not mean that writing was unknown to our great ancestors. God Brahama himself had revealed Brahmi language script, which is said to be the mother of Sanskrit and thus Sanskrit is acknowledged by scholars to be the most perfect language, with its own script. However the Vedas were not entrusted to be written on paper, parched leaves or stone because all these materials are open to obliteration due to climatic conditions, and the ravages, of time. The scriptures have persisted down the ages because our Rishis understood the superiority of mind over matter as the proper means for permanent transmittal. Mind is the most wondrous computer, If modern computers can have vast, memory, the human mind is certainly its master.

I-Tsing, the Chinese scholar who had visited India in 17th century has written that, "The four vedas containing about 100,000 verses, have been handed down from mouth to mouth, not transcribed on paper or leaves. In every generation there existed bright and intelligent Brahmins who could recite those verses verbatim. The unique fact is that in Sanskrit recitations, the second or subsequent line automatically flows down in memory, otherwise the first or single line recitations loose sense or meaning".

In Sanskrit, each character carries a fixed and invariable pronunciation. George Bernard Shaw has written a wise and witty essay on the phonetic inadequacy of Latin based English alphabet, in which the twenty six letters struggle unnecessarily to bear the burden of sound. With his customary ruthlessness, Mr. Shaw has urged a new alphabet of forty two characters. — Wilson's The Miraculous birth of Languages.

Hand made paper from specially treated woods were used for writing. Nearchus, Alexander's admiral in 4th century B.C. has written that Hindus wrote on fine tissues which were closely woven. The recent discovery of seals in the Indus Valley is leading several scholars to abandon the current theory that India had borrowed Sanskrit alphabet from Semitic sources. All these unassailable facts and evidences establish the superiority of our cultural heritage. Sanskrit is the one common national inheritance of India. The South and North, The West and East have contributed equally to it. No part of India can claim its exclusive possession. When we talk of our national genius being unity in diversity, of the fundamental oneness of Indian mind etc. what we really mean is the dominance of Sanskrit, which over-rides the regional differences and linguistic peculiarities and achieves a true national character in our thoughts and emotions and gives form and shape to languages. The basic reason for widest acceptance of Sanskrit by all the Rishis and Seers is that they had ascribed spiritual power/energy to each alphabet, which when uttered as prescribed, materialised in fulfilling the seeker's urge for blessings.

* * *

YOGI — RISHI

"tapasvibhyōdhiko yogi, gyānibhyopi matōdhikā:
karmibhyāschādhiko yogi tasmādyogi bhavārjuna:"

Shree Krishna implores Arjun to become a true Yogi

saying that a Yogi is superior to ascetics, superior to men of knowledge even, he is also superior to ritualists. The Sanskrit word Yogi means one who is joined to GOD.

It is the duty of every person to choose an ideal for his life lest he drifts and deviates into purposeless existence. An ideal ceases to be an ideal when achieved, therefore, the higher the ideal it becomes harder to achieve it; even so, one must fix an attainable ideal. The path that leads to ideals is that of a yogi who consciously and deliberately progresses towards divinity which is the purpose of Creation. With yogic advance his mind gets purified and he becomes a Siddha saint.

An ascetic is one who undergoes voluntary sacrifices in order to obtain celestial powers. What is the good of mere book reading? The learned may at best be adepts in aptly quoting from scriptures. However lifelong repeating and reciting them brings no real change or sublimation in life. What is written in the scriptures must be practiced regularly for spiritual progress; mere scriptural knowledge is of no avail to worldly wise men or women. All those who practice meditation, concentration and purification of their mind and bodily senses are real Yogis. There is no higher state than this because every thing that they undertake is worship of GOD "satatam yogi".

To explain in worldly terms, those who may have long hairs, and a flourishing beard, and wear saffron or white robes do not become Yogi. Rishis had ordained that one must remember GOD in every moment of his existence. In Maharashtra (India) a potter — Gora Kumbhar used to make pots with such great devotion that the sound of AUM used to emanate from his pots as well. Every morning one brushes teeth, washes mouth not only to eat delicious dishes but keeps his mouth clean because GOD sitting in his heart speaks through his mouth. The Rishis have said that only the man who is more competent, more enlightened and more devoted to righteousness, attains success and rises above contemporaries in this world.

The phrase "Live and let live" is wrongly used. Generally speaking it means all must enjoy the right to live. Rishis differentiated and clarified it to mean that if all assert to live then the world will collapse due to chaos because it is against the scheme of Nature. The bigger fish eats up the smaller ones; The mother snake eats up its progene soon after their birth; A tiger instinctively kills its prey but human beings are blessed by GOD to discriminate between good and bad, worthy and unworthy. Rishis emphasised that man must help man and cooperate for progress instead of wasting time and energy in gossip, bitterness, acrimony, hatred or enemosity; better encourage brotherhood, and guide the willing persons to become Yogis progressively.

* * *

AURA, HALO, PRABHĀMANDAL

Mother nature provides a protective armour of energy around the body of all objects — buildings, plants, animals, human beings etc. This is their aura. The pictures of GODS, Siddha Saints have a radiating circle of aura around their face. The aurā beams keep changing in their radiation intensity and hue with every subtle change in thoughts, emotions or passions. The aura of saintly persons remains bright white, signifying peace, tranquility and affection. This reflection becomes visible through facial expressions. Such souls have a smiling, blissful face. The warriors or persons burning with rage have red face. One can alter his/her aura as required by the situation; so long as one is alive.

American scientist Dr. Richard Green had dissected the brains of some persons and found that dismembering of some portions of brain had decreased the intensity of their desires but not motivated or obliterated them completely; This fact proved that the energy manifestation was under the control and guidance of some super-natural elements. The Sankhya Yoga system of mental modifications and characteristics of Buddhi or intellect, AHANKAR- egoism and sense consciousness are subjects of deep interest for every seeker. Rishi Kanād known as atom eater was the great discoverer of atomic individuality which became known as VAISESIKĀ science. Some relevant portions of Vaisesikā are being deeply studied.

Russian scientist Dr. Davidowich Kirliyan had developed a camera to take pictures of human aura; He took pictures of the patients and noticed disturbances in their aura. In fresh dead bodies his camera showed the aura leaving and hovering over the dead body; The aura kept diminishing and finally disappeared totally after the third day of death. This revelation confirmed the scientific basis of disposal of dead bodies by cremation lest the powerful aura of the dead person causes undesired disturbance at the home or grave-yard.

Rishi Charak and Rishi Sushruta have written and described in their medicinal volumes that every person has upto 1,000 energy points in the body. This truth has been proved by Russian Scientist Dr. Grechko Edramechow who has developed a machine fitted with photo-sensitive electric bulbs. As soon as a person stands in the machine, the photogenic bulbs start glowing nearest to the energy points in the body of that person. A hospital has been established at Vancouver and another in California, U.S.A. to treat the patients and teach them how to regulate and develop their AURA for their spiritual upliftment and self-management of their emotions/passions.

Rishi Patanjali Yoga-Sutra describes such metaphysical achievements as Animā Siddhi — extra sensory perception or micro-PSI in science. In general terminology the same phenomena is called the human aura. Scientists have probed this phenomena and have established that aura can be changed. This discovery also proved that every atom and every molecule in Nature is a continuous broadcasting station. Thus even after death, the substance that was in some living form continues to emit its delicate rays. The wave length of these rays range from shorter than anything to the longest kind of radio frequencies. The jumble of these rays is still an inconceivable enigma for the modern scientist; A single molecule may radiate one million different wave lengths at the same time. The basic difference is that radio transmitted waves get lost into oblivion but light rays keep remitting and emitting the message for countless years like echo, so scientists are endeavouring to capture the commands of Napoleon; If and when they succeed, it shall become easy to hear and compile the lost Vedas and other literary treasures of the world.

GOD SHIVA could see all this with HIS eye; Rishis and Yogis made forecasts by energising their AGYA -CHAKRA, their broadcasting apparatus of thoughts. When any feeling or thought is imprinted deeply on the heart, it acts as a mental radio and by telepathy the thoughts of one person get transmitted to another through the subtle vibrations of ether in cosmos and thereafter they come through a grosser earthly ether creating electrical waves, which in turn translates into matter or desired results.

For enlightenment and spiritual progress Rishis have laid down moral codes for purity of thoughts and actions. These are indispensable disciplines for spiritual explorations and investigations. Modern Western psychology concerns itself with subconscious mind and with mental diseases through psychoanalysis unfathomable values and powers are yet to be attained. During the last one thousand years many enlightened and self realised saints have visited Western Countries several times. Some have established their Ashrams and have gathered large followings there so, in near future we can hope for a true and genuine revival of oriental wisdom.

Saints of all religions recommend that human beings must remain for as long as possible, within the orbit of positive energy currents, so they made it obligatory for disciples to remain in the vicinity, preferably within the campus of a temple, church, gurudwaras, mosque, stupa or pagoda etc. These holy abodes have the electrical potentiality of seventy mili-volts corresponding to 11000 Bovis + +. Some prominent Hindu temples have almost the whole township inhabiting the campus. The Vatican is another good example. Pious souls visiting such places experience the bliss of these positive vibrations/currents. Hindu devotees take many rounds of their deity's sanctorum and thus they remain within the energy orbit for longer time. There is no limit for progress and attainments in spirituality for right followers.

On 4th May 1977 Cosmonaut Edgar Michael — pilot of the Apollo 14 spacecraft had given a talk at Hotel Taj Mahal, in Bombay on "Yoga and its potentiality to reveal metaphysical truths". He had said that by using telepathy he had sent messages on earth to some of his near and dear ones which had been received accurately by them. On his return to earth, he established "Institute of Nautical & Theological Sciences". He revealed that Russia is by far advanced and ahead of USA in metaphysics. Three books -- Psychic Warfare; The Mind Race and Mind Wars are published in USA on this subject. He said that USA is spending over 10 million dollars on research. In Columbia 5000 students are learning Pranayam daily.

✳ ✳ ✳

MANTRA TANTRA YANTRA

India's spiritual and cultural heritage is equally close to the hearts of men and women all over the world because Indian VEDANT emphasises man's development of total excellence. India has climbed the heights of great experience. Rishis tackled life as a whole from all aspects and gave a clarion call:

"Uttisthat jagrut prapya varannibodhat."
"Arise, awake and enlighten yourself by approaching learned souls."

The first actual contact and interaction of human beings must have been with Light, Darkness, Heat, Sound, Wind & Water. Amongst these, elements sound and light gave maximum happiness in life. The Mantra is a potent chant, a vibratory utterance in praise of the deity; The Tantra is the process/procedure of attaining the fruits of Puja or worship or Sādhanā; and the Yantra is a sketch — AKRUTI as visualised by the devotee of his deity for the purpose in his mind. The Literal translation of Mantra, Tantra and Yantra is instruments of thought, signifying the ideal, inaudible sounds which represent the desired aspect of creation when vocalised as syllables. Mantra-Tantra-Yantra constitute universal terminology. The infinite powers of sound derived from AUM. Folk lore of all people contain references to incantations with power over Nature.

The root of word Yantra is YAM which means to retain. An accurately prepared and properly propitiated Yantra retains the energy and potency of the propitiated deity. Just as a soul is encased in a human body or the flame of a wick is encased in wax (candle). Similarly, Yantra has the potency of the wick of the deity. In occult science triangles having an apex on top and also at the bottom are drawn. The pinnacle — apex triangles represent fire, SHIVA or male formation; The downwards apex triangles represent water, Nature, gravitational energy. The starting point of Creation is the conjunction and union of such triangles. A circle represents wind or space, full, complete or zero.

A mere loud utterance is no Mantra-Tantra. The chant must be inspired from within to yield desired result. The heart and soul of the devotee should become one with the deity and he should forge and loose his/her identity and become merged with the deity:

"ucharyamana ye mantra na mantrashchapi ta bindu: audo bhagwan shabda rashi: sarve varna shivatmaka."

"Correctly uttered words have the effect of being Mantra; whatever is not uttered like a Mantra is zero because every alphabet/word represents deity — Shiva." All alphabets are descriptive of the worshipped deity. In the chant many words of different alphabets reveal the cumulative potency of concerned deity. Initially the chant remains confined to the praise of deity, but with the blessings of a Siddha Guru the devotee can identify with the deity. The ultimate oneness of the Mantra-Deity-Devotee is the successful, fruitful performance, the secret of success. In each breath inhaling and exhaling, the sound of AUM should be blended; Devotee should enjoy the melody of the chant in every breath.

Great Rishi Bhrigu had compiled a large volume of Mantras in Bhrigu-Sanhitā, detailing the ups and downs in the life of every human being and forecasting their destiny, diseases, companionships, remedies etc. The Sanhita was written in coded language just as Nostradamus has written his prophesies about all world events in times to come. The mystry lies in the fact that the original script has many different key-notes called Seed- Mantras. Just as a gardener cannot claim that every seed sown by him will sprout despite his best attention and care, similarly, every Pundit or worshipper cannot claim that his version will come true or materialise. The surest thing is to have full confidence and faith in one's own self; Learn the skill from an enlightened Guru and do the performance under his auspicious guidance for positive results.

In 1919, the discovery of the radio microscope had revealed a new world of unknown ŞUN rays. This instrument could see and show, ''Man himself as well as all kinds of inert matter constantly emitting electrical rays.'' Those who believed in telepathy, second sight and clairvoyance or occult science, found scientific proof of the existence of invisible rays which travel from person to person or matter to matter. The radio is a frequency spectroscope. It does the same thing for cool, non-glowing matter that the spectroscope does when it discloses the kind of atom that make up the stars. With the discovery of the TOP-QUARK at the Fermy Labs. USA, physicists probing matter now feel that they have found the ultimate building block of the Universe. Scientists agree that clairvoyants may have seen this quark before the dawn of nuclear era.

Dr. Annie Besant and C W Leadbeater had described the minutest details of an atom in their publication — Occult

Chemistry. Both these great souls had acknowledged that they were trained by their Eastern Gurus to develop psychic powers so that they could enter an altered state of minutest consciousness in which dynamic mental images of minutest objects like atoms could be magnified. Swamy Muktanand was contacted by Neil Armstrong, the first cosmonaut to land on the moon, to describe all that he had seen on moon's surface; Swamy Muktanand went into a trance and after a little while revealed that during his transcendental meditation he had mentally visited the planet moon, and he vividly described all that the cosmonaut had seen there.

Rishi Patanjali's YogSutra describes such achievements as ANIMA Siddhi — extra sensory perception or Micro-PSI in science. In general terminology the same phenomena is called human aura or the existence and emission of such rays by all living beings in differing degrees. Scientists have probed the phenomena and have established that human aura can be changed by experts or masters. In the USA they have established two hospitals in California and Vancouver where diseases are treated by aura changes of the patient.

The great sages of India had expounded that the mind takes four forms, each with a different function. When the mind is filled with thoughts it is called 'Manas'; When it contemplates, it is called 'Chitta'; When it makes decisions it is called 'Buddhi' or intellect and when it takes on the feeling of "I"-ness, it is called Ahankar-ego. Together these 4 functions are called the 'Antahkarna' or inner psychic instrument.

Human aura is dynamic energy which changes with the mood and behaviour of every individual and indicates higher spiritual position at any given time. Human organism radiates psychic energy — a field of super-sensitivity surrounding the body. Tarun Puri runs celestial Dimensions Enterprises in Vancouver, Canada. He runs workshops also on energy awareness.

A branch of modern science — geobiology has much to reveal about the formidable knowledge known as Geomancy. Dr. E Hartmann, a German physicist has developed an instrument to identify a grid of energy lines emanating from the earth's surface and circumspecting the globe. A few important diagrams of Chakras/Yantras are appended with brief explanatory notes. Proper and accurate Yantras can be prepared by an expert and a specialist with the blessings of a Siddha Saint.

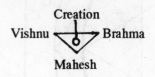

1. Combination of point (Bindu) and a triangle indicate Brahma, Vishnu and Mahesh and creation as focalpoint.

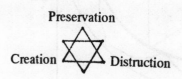

2. A hexagonal-2 triangles overlapping each other indicate Brahma, Vishnu, Mahesh, Surya (Sun), Ganesh and Durgā (Shakti). It is a combination of Shiva+Shakti. The upward apex indicates Purush the downward apex indicates Stree (female).

NAV KONATAMAK CHAKRA

3. Represent Nav-Grahas prominent planets revolving on their own axis in the Solar System.

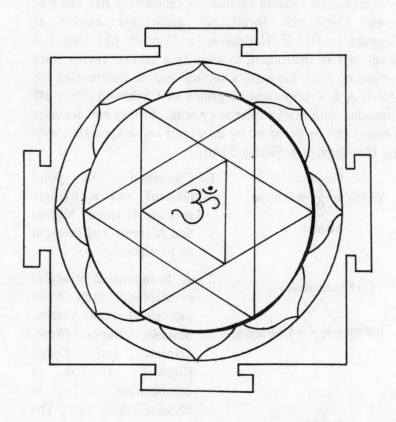

Shri Maha Ganpati Yantra
(Yantra of Lord Ganesh)

4. Shree Maha Ganpathi Yantra. A properly drawn and sanctified Yantra, if worshipped daily by a pious devotee it can fulfill all pious wishes.

5. Shree Durgā Maha Yantra. For invoking Aadi-Shakti for every success, victory and prosperity.

6. Shree Sudarshan Chakra. This Chakra is the invincible weapon of Vishnu and ShreeKrishna with miraculous powers of remote control of operation and a safe return after accomplishing assigned task.

7. Shree Chakra Or Shree Yantra. Yantra to propitiate Goddess of Wealth. A detailed note about Sudarshan Chakra and Shree Chakra is dealt with in a separate chapter.

Specimen of a few Chakra — Diagrams are appended. These are mere sketches; The properly drawn Chakra must have inscribed or written the alphabet, the name, designation and praise of the concerned deity. Then the Yantra is sanctified by a Siddha Saint who charges the potency in the Yantra with correct and clear pronunciations and recitations/hymns. Rishis had observed that different sounds generated different reactions in differing situations/circumstances. They also found that every human being has his/her individual melody and expression and each one can attain solicited virtue by his/her own personal effort and practice. They also noticed that mechanical sound did not stir up the vibrations as required. This gave birth to developed musical instruments with strings and wires so that the ringing sound could echo the desired notes, strains and appeals. For war-like preparations Nagārās, Damdamās, Bhēri, Damru, Turhi, Conch Shell etc. were used.

SHREE SHREE DURGA SAPTSHATI
MAHA YANTRAM

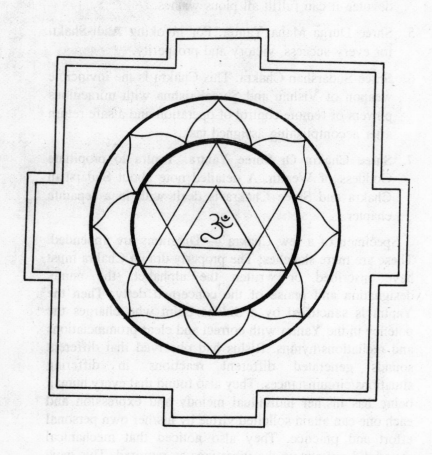

This is a special Durga Yantra indicating the Union of Shiva by
Apex upwards showing the Purush and Shakti with 2 triangles
with downward apex showing the Female Shakti with the focal
point and Aum

For appealing music, the Bānsuree, Flute, Veenā, Sitār, Sārangi, Santoor, Ektāra, etc. came in vogue.

For worship the blowing of a conch, ringing of a bell, the beating of alloy metal plates, Jhānja, Majeera etc. were recommended in accompaniment with drum, Mridangam, Tabla, Dholki etc.

For charging the Yantra with desired potency, the Rishis had also prescribed its proper Puja associated with appropriate Havan or sacrificial fire, with specific number of recitations of hymns or Shlokas by a Siddha Saint and thereafter the devotee was expected to worship that Yantra daily with absolute devotion/confidence otherwise the potency gets depleted and it might become a mere decorative piece. This explains the insistence of Rishis on performing Puja daily after a bath at a fixed place, preferably by sitting on a clean/white woolen or silk mat which should be foldedup neatly after Puja and kept separately. It need not be washed daily otherwise the energy of vibrations generated by the repeated recitations will also get washed away.

* * *

SADHANA
Transcendental Meditation

The Rishis attributed great importance to culture as well as the development of the inner faculties of human life. After countless years of experiments and progressive experiences, they developed a special system of exercises for increasing the strength, purity and power of all the faculties.

Having established the fundamentals of the functioning of the human body, they discovered various methods of feeding, resting and revitalising the body. The Rishis claimed that GOD could be attained through meditation because the mind eventually surrenders to a thought to which it is subjected without interruption for long periods. Shree Rāmkrishna Param Hansa used to say, "The mind is like a laundered cloth which takes the colour of the dye in which it is dipped. Even average mind, if dipped in the devotion of GOD, will take on spiritual colours."

Every religion has its own mythology, rituals, philosophy and higher spiritual disciplines. All forms of training, whether physical, intellectual or spiritual, are manifestations of meticulous adherance with a zeal for progress. In transcendental meditation, the performer attains a state of communion with his deity. Rishi Kapil and Rishi Pātanjali had developed and propounded in detail the psychological aspects of meditation. In the post —

Buddhist era, Shankaracharya, Ramanujacharya and others have expounded the science of Turiya-Samadhi — transcendental meditation. It is a state of going much beyond material infinity — the void beyond all forms and attributes. This is the negation of every thing conceivable or expressive. The Upnishads describe it as nor this, nor that, because the universe and mind, both are limited but the spirit of infinity, the $\overline{\text{ATMA}}$ or Brahma, is the real and true Infinity or Mounism (silence of speech).

After birth, every child sees worldly things around him and seeks comfort and happiness in them. Eventually, he develops the irresistible desire to possess them. The mind strenuously desires to acquire them but does not succeed in doing so. Failure and exasperation grips him. The child feels disappointed and this frustration pulls him closer to his objects of enjoyment. The Rishis had realised that only when we succeed in ridding ourselves of our dominant desires, does the mind become comparatively quiet. This realisation established the fact that the mind is a very changeable entity. The Rishis also discovered that no desired condition lasts long, so, by perseverance and concentration they reached a single-pointed stage and attained a condition where the worldly things lost their influence over thoughts. Thus meditation became a sublime routine.

Muslims are known for their punctuality in their Namaz -- holy prayers. There is no justification for anyone to say that he has no time to meditate. The mind tricks every person in many different directions like a vicious horse which kicks, rises on hind legs and attempts to dislodge the rider, but if the rider manages to remain stable in the saddle, the horse quietens down and starts respecting the master. An egoistic man said, ''There is NO GOD; That he himself is GOD; but if there is a GOD then he cannot escape HIS will.''

''jantunām nara janma durlabham
mamvartamānānuvartantē manusha nā hi manushāt
shreshthataram hi kinchit:''

The Rishis said that, ''In this animal kingdom, birth as a human being is the most precious gift of GOD so, all human beings must live a pure life, a holy life''. The three most important attainments in life are memory, power and quiet (peace). Every one needs a sharp memory to be able to discriminate and choose the best. A man must have food to gain strength and rest (sleep) for the rejuvenation of vitality to face the struggles of daily life. The Rishis said that for sublimation and evolution, every person must meditate on GOD atleast three times a day. The Rishis associated these three times with the SUN. When one gets up from sleep, he must pay homage to his deity or the rising SUN to prepare for the day's chorus. He must respect the mid-day SUN when he prepares to eat meals for his sustenance and the setting SUN to express his gratitude to the Creator for the successful completion of day's work and pray for restful sleep to be able to rise next morning with renewed vigour.

The Rishis proclaimed that the most auspicious time for meditation is around 3 am every day because, at that hour, Mother Nature is most serene. It is called Brahma Muharata. They also warned that if a righteous person, a Yogi slips from Yoga, he is reborn in the family of the pure and prosperous, or he is born in a family of enlightened

Yogis only. However, birth like this is very rare to obtain. In such holy family, he regains the knowledge acquired in his previous births and strives for perfection. Swami Vivekānand and his Guru Swami Rāmkrishna were perfect Yogis. The former was born in the house of a pure and prosperous family and the latter in a family of holy Yogis.

In order to attain spiritual progress, one must try to dissociate from worldly attachments. For this purpose, the Rishis advocated meditation at a predetermined place, hour and location for accelerated concentration. To make this easier, they built temples — highly energised holy places.

The Rishis learned the self-satisfying values of SA DHANA by observing the activity of the king-fisher bird who keeps sitting patiently, quite unconcerned about the surroundings on a river bank yet keenly observing the fast swimming fish in the waters. On seeing a fish within its reach, it leaps, picks up the fish, gobbles it, takes a dip in the water as if to purify itself and returns to the banks. A really good Sadhak does precisely the same practice. He concentrates all his energies on self-realisation and finds supreme bliss called the Turiya state of meditation.

* * *

HAVAN YAJNA SACRIFICIAL FIRE

All world religions have worshipped fire as a most benevolent element. From times immemorial the sacrificial fire has been the most important item of our heritage. Every auspicious function, ceremony, worship or Pujā starts with fire in some form or the other. Every religious house-holder performs a small HAVAN every morning/evening  in his residence or performs Ārti of the deity with a special deepak (lamp) a candle or incense sticks. The importance of HAVAN has been mentioned in all Vedas and other religious books. The purpose of performing Havan and related rituals has been the fulfilment of some materialistic desire or for expressing gratitude to GOD and the elements for fulfilment of cherished desires/blessings/boon.

Modern men regard HAVAN or YAJNA as a primitive practice of camp- fire, but this is the sad result of ignorance about the procedure and potency of HAVAN. Scientists have now established that even with a small domestic Havan, performed daily, preferably with cow's ghee (boiled and filtered butter) and other specified ingredients produce, while sizzling/burning valuable and purifying gases

Ethylene oxide, propylene oxide, formaldehyde, butapropiolactone and acytelene purifying gases for good health and boost up the spirits of the performer and the surroundings. Just as an injection into the body yields better/quicker result than oral medicine; similarly the subtle mix of gases produced by HAVAN mix with the blood of the performer and other inmates and grant good health.

Ignorant persons consider it wasteful to burn ghee, grains and other ingredients, but scientists have proved beyond any doubt that the ashes of HAVAN mix well with the soil and increase the field productivity manifold because the burnt ingredients preserve the traces of their properties in a suitable form to mix well with the soil. In certain medicines also the doctors prescribe minerals converted into powders of digestible/absorbent form, and these medicines are considered to be more potential than ordinary powders.

Foster the GODS through sacrificial fires and GODS shall foster you. By fostering one another without a selfish motive, one attains the greatest good. Fostered by sacrifice, the GODS certainly bestow on the devotee all that he covets, seeks, desires. He who enjoys the blessings bestowed on him, without fulfilling reciprocal obligations is undoubtably a cheat. — Gita. Ch. 3, 11/12 verse.

Rishis performed HAVAN as well as other rituals in their Ashrams (campus) with the sole aim of invoking divine blessings for the good of the society and the sound waves of the chants of Mantras, associated with the gases produced by HAVAN used to purify the total atmosphere, and ensure good health and prosperity.

Rishis performed HAVAN or YAJNA themselves for the good of society as a whole, or at the request of the king, or a leader or trader and others with a limited objective. Just as a high power broad-casting station spreads the generated waves far and wide, similarly, the chants and the gases helped the society or the person for whose benefit the performance was undertaken.

Broadly speaking, HAVANs of 14 different classifications used to be performed viz. for wealth, prosperity, good health, victory over the enemy, celebrations of victory or fulfilment of desire as thanksgiving ceremony, invoking heavenly blessings for good rain-fall, a bountiful crop, peace in times of turmoil or disharmony etc. The most vital Havan was for salvation.

Besides twigs and the dried leaves of selected/prescribed trees, the other ingredients of HAVAN are TIL-oil-seeds, barley, rice, wheat, sugar or gur, dry fruits, coconuts, raisins, Agar, Guggul, saffron musk, vermillion, turmeric as well as the dry timber of specified trees. These substances, when burnt in the fire in well graduated/regulated quantities with every chant of selected Mantra, together with spoonfulls of ghee release smoke with gases rich in beneficial properties. Repeat HAVANs multiply the potency. A HAVAN is the best and most economical means of purifying environmental pollution. Guggal and camphor are very potential germs killers. With accompanying chants and the blowing of conch, bell or drum etc. The effectiveness of the gases become manifold. Ghee particles freeze faster than water particles. The principle was to create coolness underneath the clouds so that the clouds gather closer and generate strong wind and rain.

Modern scientists have created artificial rainfall by spraying some chemicals at high altitudes to mix with the clouds and induce their bursting for desired rainfall. Thus, they determined the area where rain was required urgently. Besides helping and nursing the standing crops, the rains also wash away the rubbish and cleanse the whole area and the atmosphere in general, thus creating conditions for good health and fresh environment. Above all, the purpose performance of sacrificial fire is to produce a sweet aroma which pleases the performer and helps him in identifying himself with the performance, puts his whole heart and soul in the proper progress and culmination of the HAVAN. Such single- minded concentration yields materialising effects. The best time for performing a Havan is either morning or evening. The Tantriks prefer to perform their YAJNA at midnight, nearest to a cremation ground.

Care must be taken in performing the HAVAN with highest level of cleanliness and purity. The chants must be correctly uttered, otherwise any incorrect pronunciation or slip or mix-up can bring about undesired results which can cause irreparable harm.

The most popular YAJNA was ASHVAMEDHA whereby GOD used to be propitiated to announce that the performing king is the monarch of all he surveys and no one dared to challenge his authority; The other YAJNA, usually performed by householders was for GOD or the chosen deity to bless the devotee with children called Putreshthi-Yajna. Mostly Havans were performed for worldly gains, excepting those which used to be performed by Rishis daily for the well-being of the society in general and their own salvation.

* * *

THE MYSTIC ROMANCE OF SOME CELESTIAL FIGURES

To know what is auspicious or inauspicious, astrology and numerology can provide an answer. Some people believe that numbers have occult powers to predict future events and influence the course of life. Since antiquity, man has tried to understand the mystery of numbers. Pythagoras is considered to be the originator of numerology; But the Aryans knew all about numbers and their potency. Saint Leelavati is credited to have given the use of '0' (zero) to the world to establish distinction and correlation between divine and mundane aspects. Each number has a potency under different zodiacal influences for a good or evil effect on a person's destiny. Some numbers are considered to be beneficial others harmful. No. 13 is considered to be inauspicious. This number is ascribed to Judas who had betrayed Jesus Christ and was the 13th person at the last supper. There is no explanation for a few numbers having stigma attached to them — Nos. 10 and 420 are associated with cunning and fraud.

In Hinduism the number 108 is considered to be a holy number. A person breathes 21,600 times in 24 hours; When divided by 2 it becomes 10,800 resembling 2 horizons — the North and south Poles, emphasising 108 as basic. The sky is divided into 27 Nakshtras, each having 4 sectors of 30° each i.e. 27 x 4 = 108. The moon crosses 1 Nakshtra in 54 hours which, if divided into day and night, gives 54 x 2 =

108. Hindu rosary beads add upto 108; the significance is that 1 stands for Braham, 0, for universe and 8 for Maya (worldly illusions). The No. 1 is basic, without which nothing develops or multiplies; No. 8 is Maya which keeps growing or diminishing as in table of 8, so Braham decided to remain at a distance from Maya; when Maya combines with Braham and endeavours to become one with Braham then it neither grows nor diminishes as in the table of 9.

Similarly No. 3 is also universally applauded. AUM is a combination of 3 letters; So is GOD; For muslims the 3 letter word is Amin — phonetically, yet everybody worships only one Almighty. For Hindus No. 3 represents the Holy Trinity; Father, Son and Holy Spirits in Christianity represent number 3.

The Jews consider 613 as a sacred number; Their prayer shawl is woven with 613 threads representing 613 Torah of their holy book. The sum total of 613 is 10 i.e. Brahama, because 0 has no value of its own.

In Sikhism the number 5 enjoys reverence; Initiation into the Sikh religion is accomplished by 5 Vanies (hymns) and Kirtan is concluded by 5 Pauries.

The Muslims consider 786 as very sacred in the name of Allah, the merciful.

The Christians symbolise Jesus Christ with 888 which stands for completion, justice and fate; the Devil's number is 666.

Strangely enough, No. 13 is shunned universally, but women in Belgium wear it as talisman and a charm for good luck. Thus, it is all a matter of faith which cannot be analysed or reasoned.

The arithmetical knowledge of Rishis was of the highest order. In the Kaushitaki Brahamana the precise astronomical passages written around 3100 B.C. shows that the Hindus were far ahead in astronomy. They could calculate and indicate correct auspicious time for astrological or ceremonial occasions.

In an article, published in East-West Journal, February 1934 issue, it is printed that, "Jyotish or Vedic astronomical treatises contain scientific lore which kept India at the forefront of all ancient nations and made her the Mecca of seekers after knowledge." Brahamagupta, a treatise on astrology, is replete with astronomical data dealing with such matters as helio-centric motion of planetory bodies in our solar system. The obliquity of the ecliptic, the earth's spherical form; The reflected light of moon; The earth's daily axial revolutions, the presence of fixed stars in the Milky Way; The law of gravity and other scientific facts which did not dawn on the Westerners until the time of Copernicus & Newton."

The Arabic numerals, considered most valuable in Western mathematics, had actually reached Europe in the 9th century, via Arbistan, from India, where that system of notation had been followed and formulated ages ago. Modern scholars are told that Arabs and Greeks learnt the use of '.' decimal point and '0' zero from the great Indian mathematician — Leelavati. Now, the west has acknowledged that India was the first nation to send and establish a satellite Arya Bhatt in space.

Shri Ramanujam was a great scholar of mathematics and last year, another learned scholar, who was put behind bars by unaccountable government and remained imprisoned for several months, has solved a mathematical problem over which the world mathematicians were puzzled; This scholar has established that with the help of book Leelavati, all mathematical problems can be solved easily, speedily. Dr. Narlikar and others are carrying the Bhartiya torch of light to enlighten and illuminate the world's progress. Further information can be gathered from Sir P C Roy's book, History of Hindu Chemisry; In B N Seal's — Positive Science of Ancient Hindus; and in B K Sarkar's — "Hindu Achievements in Exact Science; Also in "The Positive Background of Hindu Sociology" and many other books and volumes. An organisation established at Choukhambā, in Vāranasi (India), has collected many old manuscripts, palm-leaves writings, and they are busy in compiling the lost treasures of knowledge.

* * *

GOD SUN
Giver of life & vigour

"surya ātmā jagtasthushsch yadāditya gatam tejō
jagadbhāsayatē akhilam"

SUN is the soul of whole universe; SUN is the source of life for all living beings.

Rishis had made a detailed study of the effects and benevolence of the SUN GOD for countless number of years and arrived at fascinating conclusions. SUN has a bright saffron-cum-vermilion glow early morning and in the evening. At noon it looks like a fire-ball; Its temperature varies during different

months and seasons of every year; It helps the growth and development of every thing on earth; It emits short and long rays of seven different vibrations of varying intensity; Chemical changes are brought about by SUN rays in matter, water and air etc.

The SUN is the preserver and protector of life on earth. Above all RISHIS discovered that SUN rays build strong bones, increase vitality and thus protect human beings from several diseases so they started worship of SUN and composed prayers, called Gayatri: "Aum bhu: Aum bhuva: Aum swa: Aum maha: Aum jana: Aum tapa: Aum satyam; Aum tatsaviturvarenyam bhargo devasya dhimahi, dhiyoyona: prachodayāt Aum."

"We pray and pay homage to HIM who is the creator and preserver of universe; He loves and protects all; Our whole body radiates with ecstasy owing to HIS powers, energy, potency and keeps us free from fear and vices and increases our brilliance".

Amongst Hindus a Guru initiates a disciple by reciting the above sanskrit mantra into his ears and performs the sacred thread ceremony; This is considered to be the second birth of the disciple as an intellctual. The spiritual guru teaches the disciple the correct and appropriate utterance and pronunciation of this very potential mantra and explains in detail the benevolent effects of reciting this mantra at different hours of the day, in different seasons. Thus for a scientist or an astronomer the SUN is just a huge fire-ball emitting heat currents but (Rishis had established that SUN is a real, never resting, life force. Our whole life and existence depends on SUN.

It is unbelievable that water can be found on the burning hot SUN, but chemists and star gazers have discovered water not in the hot gaseous heart of SUN itself, but on some cooler spots of SUN. Peter Bernath a research scientist has said, "Hydrogen and oxygen molecules both exist on the SUN which is about 10,200°F (5,700°C). They apparently combine to form water on Sunspots which are about 5,200°F (2,900°C)."

Rishis announced that the rising SUN as well as the

setting SUN regulates the day and night; divides the year into 12 months of six different seasons by moving from North Pole to South Pole and vice versa. They gave different names to SUN according to its effectiveness for every month of the year and the season.

"a pachitā prapatat suparnō vaste ravi: Surya kranotu bheshjam Chandramā vopochhtū."

SUN helps the growth of different life giving herbs and the MOON helps humanity in getting rid of body ailments. This truth is proved by peasants who remain healthy and strong even without enjoying two square meals a day because they are blessed by the SUN and the MOON all the year round. Westerners are now realising and recognising these truths; They derive pleasure and happiness from SUN baths.

The World Health Organisation (W.H.O.) has recognised colour therapy by harnessing rays of SUN to establish the energy level balance in the human body to get rid of ailments.

"ārogyam bhāskarādichhēnmoksh michhē janārdanāta."
An English proverb explains this Sanskrit statement as, "Light IS life; Darkness IS death". The Rishis said the same thing, "SUN grants good health" but GOD grants the liberation of soul."

Dr. E. George an American scientist, has written that to test the truth that SUN is a living GOD, one day he went up on the terrace of his bungalow and stood naked for 5 minutes at 10 am; On returning to his room he measured his body temperature and the thermo-meter read 100°F; on the next morning, he took a bath and at the previous day's time he took with him some fresh fruits, flowers and a tumblar full of fresh water on the terrace, bowed down respectfully to SUN, said his prayers for full eleven minutes, returned to his room and was astonished to find his body temperature normal at 97°F. "Faith moves mountains!"

Dr. Robert Green had established a fascinating sanatorium in 1903 at Lesin on the Alps where total treatment is given using the SUN rays. Many other doctors have adopted this therapy in USA as Naturopathy.

It is astonishing to learn that basic food for growth and development of the body is nothing but 'colour' because the vegetables or meat which people eat is concentration/condensation of different colours in varying degrees and forms. There are colours and their combinations which can keep a person sick, melancholy or even drowsy. Rishis had mastered the technique and skill of obtaining nutrition and strength by associating and assimilating different colour rays of SUN and thus brightened their intellect to enjoy a long, healthy life without eating food for several days, without any loss of vitality.

Rishi Patanjali explains the technique of acquiring Siddhis. If one meditates on an object for a long time, that object eventually disappears, the seer and the seen merge into each other; When the seer and the seen and the process of seeing become one, one obtains mastery over the object called Samyama Shakti. By Samyama concentration on an elephant one can get the strength of an elephant. By focussing attention on the SUN, one can bring its power into himself, he can see what is taking place in the entire solar system. By Samyama on the throat region, one can acquire the power to do without food or drink. Theress Neumann a simple German lady, lived without eating food for years. On enquiry, she said that she is forbidden by her Guru NOT to reveal the secret OR temper with. God's laws.

A few years ago a tribal woman of Orissa (India), was detained in judicial custody to make sure that she had attained non eating state using yogic powers; This Giribala had mastered the breathing technique to energise the Vishuddha Chakra located near the heart and just below the throat; This Chakra controls ākāsh — space which fills our body cells.

Dr. G.W. Crile of Cleveland, USA has said that, "What we eat is radiation; which releases electrical currents for the body's energy circuit, the nervous system, is given to food by SUN rays". Atoms are solar systems. Atoms are the vehicles that are filled with solar radiance as so many coiled springs. These atomfulls of energy are taken in by us as food. Once in the human body, these atoms are discharged in the body's protoplasm, the radiance furnishing new chemical energy. Our body is made up of these atoms termed as muscles, brain, and sensory organs such as eyes, ears, skin, tongue, nose etc." Laymen do not know the strides that science has taken. The Transmutation of metals and other chemical dreams are getting fulfilled in world's sophisticated laboratories. In the near future man will learn how he can live directly on solar energy.

Chlorophyll is just one substance known to scientists which acts as a sunlight trap. Dr. M. Lawrence had written in New York Times, It catches the energy of sunlight and stores it in the plant; no life could exist in its absence. We obtain solar energy from the plant and vegetation for living;

or in the meat of animals who eat plants. The energy we obtain from coal or oil is solar energy trapped by chlorophyll in plants, millions of years ago."

Rishis had learnt that the colours are just a hue of different wave-length-rays, radiating from SUN. The light that we see is only a small portion of solar radiation termed as the electromagnetic-speed of rays. Different alphabets and their correct utterances is really the speed with sound movement, generating and producing different colour impressions or visibility, thus VIBGYOR colours and 7 Swar-notes/sounds are interwoven, inter- changeable.

The French scientist Dr. M.G. Claude had given a live demonstration at Fontainebleau in 1928 before an assembly of leading world scientists, through his deep knowledge of chemistry about the transformations of oxygen. Dr. Claude explained how the sea could be turned by oxygen transformations into many million pounds of horse-power energy; how water which boils is not necessarily burning; how little sand mounds could be converted into sapphires, rubies, topaz etc. by a single whiff of oxygen; He predicted that in not too distant future man shall be able to walk on the bottom of ocean without diver's equipment. This great scientist amazed his audience by turning their faces black by taking the red out of SUN'S rays. This noted scientist produced liquid air by an expansion method by which he was able to segregate various gases of air; He has also discovered means of the mechanical utilisation of differences of temperature in sea water at different levels.

Rishis had discovered that plants are not able to absorb all the colours of SUN rays; plants could assimilate colours in varying quantities and degrees as such the stem and branches remain brown; fresh offshoots and leaves remain greenish-purple, buds, flowers and/or fruits show single or compound colours; That all flowers blossoming after sunset remained white, but those which blossomed around sunrise or during the day were a combination of deep or multi-colour hues; that some particular flowers changed their colours upto 3 times during the day with bright SUN. They also discovered that red colour rays were the longest and strongest, so they specified different coloured flowers for worship, they ordained that all Goddesses should be worshipped with red flowers. Most valiant, vigorous, brilliant and powerful GODS were also depicted in red colour and named Ganesh, Hanuman and Bhairav. The flags of these GODS and GODDESSES were also determined to be red. Thus the potency and utility of red colour was known to Rishis at the dawn of civilisation. Communists and trade-unions have adopted a red flag and red salute in recent years.

Modern scientists have found that light rays travel at a varying speed of 400 to 730 Nano-meters. 1 NM is equal to 1/100th million part of 1 meter length. Vegetation, animals and human beings see, the rays as per their visual capacity but all living beings cannot see, absorb or assimilate all the colour rays. The mixture of all 7 vibgyor rays yields a pure white colour. Total absence of light is darkness or the black colour.

Great seers and thinkers had chosen different colours depending upon their property/potency. Magicians prefer black colour or darkness to learn/display their skills. Peace loving, calm and quiet persons love white; Muslims showed preference for green colour which denotes freshness; Nihang Sikhs like blue colour because they find self-satisfaction and peace in deep blue colour denoting love for solitude. Hindus and Jains prefer a deep orange colour resembling a flame; It indicates brilliance, alertness, self-confidence and purity of thought and mind. In short, the choice or liking for any colour is indicative of that person's character, thinking and behaviour. With adequate knowledge of psychic effects of different colours and shades, parents can make their children brave, brilliant, sober, intellectual or quarrelsome and so on, provided such parents have enough time to nurse and train their children.

* * *

YOGESHWAR SHREEKRISHNA

One great characteristic of all great scriptures of mankind is that they are written in plain speech, popular in that era, but they hold profound depths of great value; The inquisitive reader feels that, "veil upon veil will lift, still there remains veil upon veil behind". The inner meaning is ever fresh and new. As we advance in experience of life, with the precepts enjoined in the scriptures, we realise that they are very true. The world is not a haphazard conglomeration of living beings lumped together to go on as per their capability or understanding; A clear, systematic, and successful plan is visible.

Modern science also admits of a purpose behind all manifestations and of a mathematical mind that guides the universe. The modern man has the tendency to disown the idea of a personal GOD. He argues that if man cannot love and serve his own brother, whom he can see, how can he serve GOD Whom he does not see? To him, GOD is his brother or nearest neighbour. Scriptures reiterate the same truth -- Supreme cometh to a man along the way he chooses "Ye yatha man prapadyante tams thaiva bhajami aham. "In whatever way men identify with Me, in the same way I carry out their desires..."

"vasudeva sutam devam kams chanura mardanam, Devaki parmanandam Krishnam vande jagadgurum. mukam karoti vachalam pangum langhayate girim; yatkrupa tam aham vande parmananda madhavam."

I salute Lord Krishna, the world teacher, the son of Vasudeva, the destroyer of Kamsa and Chanura, the supreme bliss of Devaki. I salute the Madhava, the source of supreme bliss, whose grace makes the dumb eloquent, and the cripple cross mountains.

These Sanskrit couplets start with describing blissful family bonds. To be the father of ShreeKrishna was a meritorious blessing, a heavenly boon; All sons should make their parents glorious with good deeds then alone the world shall become a heaven. Every person can not be endowed with supernatural powers yet, there remain many other virtues, qualities which men can emulate.

Wicked and sensuous rulers in those days were called ASURAS or rascals, so Krishna had to annihilate and destroy them. All living beings are, according to religious concept, Brahamkumari brides, and the Lord as the only bridegroom capable of guiding them to transcend body consciousness. The relationship between the individual soul and the cosmic reality was thus personified; Plan and Purpose of life was revealed.

Many puerile moralists hold that ShreeKrishna's relationship with numerous Gopis was scandalous. This position of pseudo-moralist arises from perverse understanding because ShreeKrishna had left Vrindavan-Nandgram at age 9 only. Is it ever possible for a young urchin to have passionate relationship with hundreds of women? The milk-maids remained faithful to their husband and family: They invited each other and all of them joined in the mirth with the divine lad. ShreeKrishna is adored as Hrishikesh — The Lord of senses, and not a slave of the senses as normal mortals are. The Gopis enjoyed beatitude in the blissful company of Krishna.

ShreeKrishna sets an example about the attitude that one should have towards one's worldly career. Long before entering youth His sprightly sports at Vrindavan had been completed. HE viewed this world as a huge playground and treated life as a delightful sport.

The period of exile for the Pandavas was over; They had faithfully fulfilled all the difficult terms imposed on them for the sin of gambling. They were entitled to receive back their empire, but the covetous Kauravas bluntly refused to part with even one inch of the territory; Conciliation seemed to be impossible. Both parties knew ShreeKrishna very well so both approached HIM to be on their side; He readily agreed to help both, on condition that Pandavas and Kauravas shall have to declare their preference; ShreeKrishna said that they were free to choose between:

(1) His total army and allied resources; OR

(2) He himself, totally unarmed on the other side.

Arjun opted to have ShreeKrishna himself on his side; Duryodhan was delighted to hear Arjun's choice because he could have claimed what Duryodhan dearly wanted; Duryodhan's faith was in the army and its mobilisation in his favour, whereas Arjun subordinated the power of army and gallantry to God's grace.

ShreeKrishna demonstrated the divine principles of life, which are irrevocably linked with progress. On a battle-field, the warrior gives his best performance to win, so ShreeKrishna chose Kurukshetra as the historic spot to rid Arjun of his perplexities. Body-centered life is itself a kind of warfare. Arjun was dead set for a deadly encounter with the wicked Kauravās. His conviction was that the man who dared to oppose him, opposed righteousness itself so, he asked Krishna to drive his chariot between the two arrayed armies to have a glance of all who were on the side of the sinful war. Krishna drove the chariot in front of Bhishma Pitāmaha and the revered Guru Dronāchārya — both were worthy of veneration to Arjun so, Arjun was on the horns of dilemma; To fight or flee, he could not decide. Finding himself of divided mind, he appealed to Krishna to guide and enlighten him and guide to tide over the suspense. On all such occasions, Krishna came to his rescue and this was the most opportune time for Geetā discourse.

To remove the despondency of Arjun, Krishna explained in detail that the Atman — soul is immortal; Feelings and emotions pertain to the body only, so be not attached to these weaknesses; swerve not from duty, transform deeds into Karm-Yoga. But Arjun remained uncertain so, to clarify the proposition from all angles, Krishna continued explaining to him the difference between deferring actions — The path of renunciation, knowledge, meditation, divine manifestation, discrimination, realisation, the sovereign science and sovereign secret, vision of cosmic form, devotion, Yoga of division of Trigunas — birth-functions-salvation etc. Shraddha-sublimation and finally the Yoga of liberation by renunciation. It must be noted that all these deep knowledges, from different angles/aspects was imported to Arjun to decide and choose his correct duty at that critical juncture.

ShreeKrishna was not preaching different philosophies nor was any comparison done to discriminate one against the other; It was just a conscience arousing chat to clear Arjun's doubts, but the exposition is so lucid and thorough that the Geeta has become the best code of conduct for every individual or society to perform all worldly duties and obligations without worldly attachment, for salvation.

ShreeKrishna clarified the abstract teachings of the Vedas and Upnishads because of Arjun's craving for enlightenment. The love of the calf induces the cow to secrete more milk, which incidentally benefits many parched palates. Geeta is an indispensable guide to every person who has the inner urge for enlightenment; Even for saints who may be nearer to their goal of salvation. Life in secular or sacred aspects gets abundantly enriched by sincere and faithful pursuit of the tenets of Geeta, hence it is called Mother.

The common notion that Vedantism is concomitant with quietude was repudiated in no uncertain terms; That passivity or escapism was blown to pieces. Equilibrium of the mind can be had as much as in a sanguinary battle-field as in the quite of a cave. ShreeKrishna sets an example for the correct attitude one should have towards one's worldly responsibilities. Positive service is rendered by the wind which brings and assembles rain-nearing clouds; whereas a dust storm makes men miserable. The Geeta is not a dust raising whirlwind; The real values of a successful life, a brilliant code of conduct for one and all is enshrined in Geeta. With love and compassion Lord ShreeKrishna imparts the knowledge of virtues, self-denial and strength to Arjun instead of pleasures that are sense-bound mutations.

Bhagwan ShreeKrishna's message is Gnyana, Bhakti and Karma — knowledge, devotion and duty. In HIS incarnation he lived upto HIS preachings so, Rishis declared "kranvanto vishwa maryam" be like Krishna. They preached not to beg for sympathy or pity or mercy, because mercy can be shown to someone other than himself. Awake, arise, identify yourself with GOD — tatva masi — thou art thee.

In this world every one has to assert for survival; He who does not know how to fight for his rights does not succeed. Even the mother does not fed her own child until he cries loudly and kicks up a row. To secure a job, a skilled person establishes his talents and dexterity. State-craft itself is a strategy in war. A resolute forward step in any field means that the person has fought for achieving success and victory. Krishna demonstrated himself how to face bewildering situations in his career. Geeta teaches one to equip oneself for winning the battle of life; His teaching is, "Fight the battle of life; Let the virtue in you vanquish the vice". The teeming bad tendencies very often outnumber the good ones; These good and bad tendencies appear to be close cousins because of their common origin. Opposed to each other as they are, these two tendencies try to dominate the very existence of man. The evil ones among them are adept at mobilising in their favour all possible resources and arguments or statistics.

ShreeKrishna is depicted as having a discus in his right hand finger and a conch in left hand. The significance of these attribute is that for the evil doers. He uses the Sudarshan Chakra — discus for eliminating them and this message is carried to all ears through blowing the conch, a contemporary sublime way for all declarations. The Mahābhārat war used to be started every morning by blowing the conch and at sunset the conch was blown again to stop warfare for the day. GOD is above any virtue or vice.

There is no need for HIM to involve HIMSELF in any action; He remains as a witness only out HIS grace always favours 'good'. ShreeKrishna's consent to become charioteer establishes his truth. HIS presence as 'conscience' within all human beings is perceptible to all who are virtuous.

As per our cultural traditions, our civilisation had started with Satya-Yug when everyone was truthful and righteous; but human nature as it is, persons of that era perhaps tried to become possessive so that muscle power became supreme in Tretā Yug when Rāmā had to take Avatār to annihilate the power drunk regime of Rāvan; Might is right was replaced by the incarnation of ShreeKrishna to spread the message of love and harmony reestablish the righteous path in DwaparYug. The wheel has moved down, persons have become egoistic again in KaliYug; the night is darkest before the dawn so even this shall not last; Wheel of Time shall move up to herald the Golden age soon.

* * *

SHREE RĀMĀ
IDEAL FOR HUMANITY

"Shri Ramāya namastubhyam naram chawa narottamam to Cebeissante Shree Rāmā".

Rishi Bālmiki desired to write an epic — a Mahā Kabya — a grand literary composition, describing the heroic deeds of an ideal human being so, he implored Rishi Nārad to tell him if he knew of such a national hero. Rishi Nārad entreated Rishi Bālmiki to write about the life and achievements of Shree Rāmā who had all the virtues of an ideal person; Virtuous, righteous, truthful, respectful, humble, humane, inspiring and handsome. In his RĀMA YAN, Rishi Bālmiki has portrayed Shree Rāma as a human being who attained Godhood by virtue of his own physical, moral and spiritual achievements; He has faithfully narrated all the events of Shree Rāma's life. In every episode, Lord Rāma never lost his cool and balance despite the onslaught of tragic situations including a ferrocious war with the demon king Rāvan which was fought by Rama without a well trained and properly gear-equipped army.

The world today yearns for reestablishment of Rāma Rājya; The world would not have known anything about the virtues and merits of Rāma Rājya if Shree Rama had conceded to his coronation ceremony, as decreed by king Dashrath, in unanimous agreement of all his cabinet members and respected leaders of society; Then it would have been just a continuation of Dashrath Rājya, administered by Shree Rāma. For common man Shree Rama had become Bhagwan Vishnu incarnate; An ideal for worship and a powerful source of inspiration for good.

The world needed Shree Rama, a mortal human being to kill the demon king Ravan because the latter; had won a boon that excepting a man no one else shall kill him. To authenticate his avatār — incarnation, as a human being Shree Rama identified his total existence as a man, his behaviour, relationships, dealings administration etc. etc.

In the following sequences Rāma has exhibited superb calm even while receiving/conveying contradictory, yet appropriate thoughts without emotional upset. He never allowed any emotion to override his balanced actions/decisions. Even in the condition of extreme distress after Sitā's kidnaping by Rāvan, Shree Rāma expressed extreme agony and cried like a mortal man, but never lost his cool; instead he vowed to make every possible effort to trace and win back Sitā.

HUMANE BEHAVIOUR

In the ferrocious battle fought on the grounds of Lankā, Rāvan had announced that if any of his soldiers attempted to run away from the battle field, he shall be treated as a betrayer and killed without mercy; Shree Rāma on the other hand invariably cheered up his injured troops and always remained at the head of the fighting units wherever required. In the final battle, the chariot and bow of Ravan became damaged so Rama stopped warfare, told Ravan to go back and return for battle in a new chariot with new weapons although Rama himself had no chariot and his bow and other weapons were intact and so Ravan could have been slain easily. Seeing this unbelievable scene everyone sang the praise of Rama, "You are supreme GOD Vishnu incarnate". Shree Rama spontaneously declared,

ātmānam manushyam manya Rāmam, Dashrathatamajam.

"No, I am also a human being, Rāma, son of king Dashrath".

HUSBAND

On hearing the proclamation about his coronation Rama felt extremely elated. In those blissful moments he felt intense joy and rushed to give this good tiding to his consort Sitā.

When Rama learnt about his banishment orders he endeavoured to dissuade Sita from accompanying him to the forests where life would be full of difficulties and discomforts.

In those days, it was a common practice amongst kings to have many queens but Rama had declared that Sita alone would be his wife, so after his victorious return to Ayodhya, the Royal Court decided to organise Ashvamedha Yagna wherein the victorious king had to sit with his wife for offerings. Shree Rama had a gold statue of Sita made instead of taking a second wife.

HUMAN RIGHTS

Rishi Vishwamitra had taken Shree Rama to his Ashram in the forest for protection of the Yagnas and the Rakshsas -- demons continued their sacrileges and the killings of Rishis unabated so Rama took a vow that he shall kill all demons. On hearing that vow, Sita pulled up Rama saying,

"You are a hermit now, and the demons have done no harm to you as such your vow to destroy them is unjust and unfair". Rama smiled and replied, "True, I am a recluse today, but I am a born Kshatriya, so it is my religious duty to protect saints, noble and/or weak persons. That is why I have brought my bow and arrows to kill the wicked demons; I shall not kill any innocent person".

PROTECTOR

Bibhishan was insulted and kicked out by Ravan from his Court — Darbār. He approached Shree Rāma to seek asylum just when the military preparations were in progress to invade Lanka. The Monkey king Sugriva and other ministers opined against granting asylum to Rāvan's real brother at that vulnerable stage; Hanuman alone commended the grant of asylum saying that during his exploratory visit to Lanka in search of Sitā, he had met Bibhishan and had found him to be helpful. Shree Rāma endorsed this broad minded and humane approach, and said "Even if Rāvan solicits my protection he shall have it; I do not turn away anyone who seeks shelter from me".

BROTHER

In Ramayan there is no episode at all indicating any quarrel of jealousy amongst the brothers. Shree Rama regarded all brothers as vital parts of his own body. All of then shared unrivalled faith/confidence and respect for each other.

On the battlefield of LANKA, Lakshman lay unconscious having been hit by Nāag-Pāsh and no medical relief was within sight. Deeply grieved Rāma said, "If I would have known that I shall loose my real brother in such a tragic situation I would have preferred to disobey my father's command to accept banishment from Ayodhya because in this world it is not possible to have such a good real brother''.

King Bharat sincerely wanted to bring back Shree Rāma from Chitrakoot mount ceremoniously, so he proceeded from Ayodhya with royal emblems, army divisions and other paraphernalia. Lakshman received the report of Ayodhya's army marching towards Chitrakoot in full formations. He could not visualise any justification for such ominous preparations so, he told Rāma, ''See, Bharat is coming with the army to annihilate us, but he seems to be sadly mistaken in believing that Shree Rāma is alone and defenceless; I vow to kill Bharat if he has any malafied intentions''. Shree Rāma counselled patience to Lakshman saying that, ''Do not get so excited; I know Bharat very well; he is coming just to meet us; better wait and watch''. And both brother were happy to see Bharat and the mothers assembled there in a homely, affectionate atmosphere. Shree Rāma went a step further and declared that, ''If dear Bharat wants me to return to Ayodhya, I shall abide by his decision despite my self-accepted banishment at the command of my parents''. There is no parallel example of such brotherly confidence and mutual respect in the world.

KING

Shree Rama is known as an ideal king who had laid down a venerable code of conduct by example and not by legislation. In those days the king was regarded as the 'father' of the total populace, so he had to be above any suspicion and most benevolent, generous and righteous. This duty of a king explains the reason why Shree Rāma agreed as king to banish Sitā because a commoner had cast doubt on the character of Sitā because of her confinement in Lanka, under the suzerainty of the vicious Rāvan.

On the battle field of Lanka, Rāvan was lying dead and his brother Bibhishan refused to perform the last rites of a cruel and demoralised person. Shree Rama said,

"marnānānti vairāni nivratamanā prayojanam kriytāmasya sanskāra: mamāpesyā yathatavamam".

"Ravan was a brave, mighty king and he had died fighting on the battle field as a brave warrior, he is no longer a wicked king so he deserves all the traditional royal respect: It is your solemn duty to perform all befitting rites: If you still decline, then I shall perform them".

POLITICS

To honour two boons which king Dashrath had given to his queen kekai; much against his wish, Dashrath condescended to banish Rama for 14 years from Ayodhya and to make her son Bharat the king. King Dashrath could not pronounce his consent of banishment so Kekai had to inform Rama of this. On hearing that decision of his father, Rama was not upset at all. Rama said, "dhāryan mansa dukham". Keeping his emotional depression under control, he went to his mother Kaushalyā to break that sad news and counselled her to accept the *fait accompli* with grace; Mother is invariably the first person interested in ever lasting well-being of her children;

Human nature is unpredictable, people may change their behaviour under the compulsions so Rāma went to Lakshman to persuade him to stay behind to look after mother Kaushalyā and Sumitrā lest the step mother Kekai might torture them out of jealousy and brother Bharat might also ignore them because power corrupts.

SECULARISM

Shree Rama had won the hearts of all who came in contact with him; He never supported or acknowledged differences due to colour, caste or creed; Instead of adhering to royal protocol he took pleasure in meeting persons who were considered to be untouchable as per the prevalent social customs.

He called on Shabri, a religious tribal woman and accepted and ate the forest berries which she had tasted and preserved for offering. Nishād Rāj Guha and boatsman Kewat were embraced by Rāma like his own brothers; On hearing about this personal gesture, king Bharat and Rishi Vashishtha also embraced Nishād Rāj and Kewat.

To fight against the powerful, and wicked demons, Shree Rāma raised an invincible army of village folk, monkeys, birds, bears, and even reptiles instead of summoning the well trained and best equipped army from Ayodhyā or Janakpur. Love is not getting but giving; It is the result of pure living without obsessions or reservations.

Thus Shree Rāma had endeared himself to all his subjects, contemporary kings and sages alike; Everyone worshipped and prayed for permission to be close to him. These virtues and humane qualities of Shree Rāma have endeared him so much that even today, the world remembers and respects him and yearns for the establishment of Rāma Rājya to be able to live happily in peace and plenty.

* * *

SHREE HANUMAN AN IDEAL FOR DEVOTION & LOYALTY

Hanuman is one of the most popular deities of the Hindu pantheon for his valour, dynamism, wisdom, presence of mind, loyalty and devotion to duty in letter and spirit. Deeds which called for the geatest courage, will-power fell to his lot and he performed them upto the last stage of success. His devotees sing in praise of him:

MANOJAVAM MĀRUT TULYA VEGAM, JITENDRIYAM BUDDHIMATĀM VARISHTHAM, VĀTĀTMAJAM VĀNAR YOUTH MUKHYAM, SHREE RĀMĀ DOOTAM, SHARNAM PRAPADHYE!!

With a smart & alert mind, you command wind-like speed, you are master of all senses (Indriyas). Highest intellect & wisdom child of Lord WIND, chief of monkeys, you are a loyal devotee of Shree Ramā, I bow down to you for your prowess! This prayer does not sing His praise for valour/courage/feats; but describes His virtues.

The gods desired to gauge the skills of Hanuman so they deputed Sursa (mother of snakes) who confronted him while he was getting ready to fly over the ocean; Hanuman politely told her, "Let me return after accomplishing Rāmā's errand and reporting to him Sitā's where abouts; hereafter I swear to return to you to make me your meal; Mother permit me to proceed..." Sursā tested Hanuman's skills and wisdom and complemented him for his presence of mind and courage.

Mythology maintains that Lord Sivā always desired to remain close to Lord Rāmā who was actually an incarnation of VISHNU so, Sivā incarnated himself as a monkey; This form was chosen by Sivā because, though inferior to a human body, a monkey has few wants, does not require clothing or shelter and is able to subsist on vegetation which is abundantly available.

Hanumān was an extra ordinary monkey with uncommon powers including a capability to fly/float in the air and assume any form worthy of the situation. This explains that a person becomes great by his deeds accomplished for the benefit of society and not merely by physical strength or intellect.

Gita also explains the same thing that professional expertise is man's way/path for Godhood; By performing one's duties efficiently, one worships GOD and becomes one with HIM.

Swami Vivekanand had said, "For next 50 years ... let all vain gods disappear from our minds. Hanuman is the only GOD vibrant and alive to every situation; All other gods are in deep slumber. What vain gods shall we go after instead of GOD who is all around us; Our real gods are men and animals around us -- the first gods we have to worship are countrymen". The whole world is GOD'S self manifestation.

Sage Nāarad has mentioned in Bhakti Sūtra, one should not argue in religious matters because there always exists scope for diversity in views; No one philosophy can be considered final based on reasoning alone -- reasoning being a faculty of Buddhi, which is not absolute. "Vado navalambyah".

INTELLIGENCE & ATTAINMENTS

Hanuman entered Lanka in a dwarf form, all the time analysing in his mind about right step at every stage. During search for Sitā, Hanumān sees many women in the palace of Rāvan, half asleep, half drunk and thought, "The mind is responsible for the functioning of all INDRIYAS (senses), but my mind is unruffled and at peace", so he did not feel shy or disturbed at all. Seated on Ashok tree he was a silent witness to Rāvan's visit and his appeals to Sitā for a kindly glance at him; ultimately when Sitā felt desperate and decided on suicide, Hanumān started narrating the happenings with Shree Rāmā and convinced her to look-up. He then consoled her and gave her the signet ring of Rāmā. Sitā was immensely pleased and blessed him profusely saying, "You are intelligent, smart, resourceful, the best amongst monkeys. You shall remain immortal and a treasure of virtues. You will enjoy affection of Shree Rāmā".

Indrajeet used Brahmāstra rendering Shree Rāmā, Lakshman and made the army unconscious. Vibhishan happened to see Jāmbavān lying almost half dead so he tried to talk and revive him; Jāmbavān spontaneously enquired whether Hanuman was alive? Vibhishan enquired, "Why are you asking for Hanuman first" and Jāmbavān replied, "If the courageous Hanuman is alive, he has the wisdom and vallour to bring back to life the entire army even if dead but if Hanuman is dead all of us are as good as dead even if alive".

Shree Hanuman had been blessed with a boon by Sitā of immortality, "So long as this world will speak about Rāmā, you will stay in this world to listen to the praise of Rāmā and the world shall be benefited with your presence". After the glorious return of Hanuman and Angad from Lanka, king Sugrivā, narrated to Rāmā all the victories and accomplishments of Hanuman; Shree Rāmā enquired as to how could he achieve such stupendous glories, Hanuman politely said, "Lord all the glory is yours, I am a simple monkey jumping from one tree to another by nature" and Lord Shree Rāmā said, "Hanuman, I am highly indebted to you for all that you have done and achieved for me."

There is no other single character in world literature, who never asked for any recognition or reward for all the heroic deeds and remained unassuming, so he is a GOD.

* * *

GOD SHIVA
(Ardhanarishwar)

God Shiva is a par excellence manifestation of wisdom, prowess, will-power, action and bounty. He wears a tiger

skin as a loin cloth and his abode is a cremation ground or Mount Kailash. He alone is known for generously giving boons of riches, possessions and power to His devotees. God Shiva combines in Himself one single entity of creator, preserver and destroyer. All these attributes are visible in His attire. He neither needs nor expects anything from His devotees. He is always ecstasy and joy personified.

Initially God Shiva was one-half male, One-half-female — Ardhnarishwar. Later God separated Himself in different forms.

Bodily Bhagwan Shankar is camphor white but His throat is blue like sapphire and the whole body beams like bright coral. He has three eyes and four hands. He is depicted as a combination of Purush and Prakriti so His ornaments are also complementary. His root (seed) Mantra — Om ram ksham mam yam om. His Gayatri Mantra is "aum tatpurishyaaya vidmahe mahadevaya dhimahi tanno rudra prachodayat".

In Sanskrit the word ling stands for rhythm and yoni for sound; The combination of rhythm and sound represents Jyotirling, or Buddhi and intellect. Thus the concentration of mind and intelligence on any sublime aspect is the real and complete worship of Bhagwan Shiva.

The great ocean churning had thrown up deadly poison and other intoxicants besides many other charming gifts. Both Gods and the demons, declined to accept poisons. If the poisons and intoxicants were allowed to spread, the whole universe would have been destroyed. So, the Gods appealed to Mahadev Shiva to spare the lives of posterity. To preserve creation, God Shiva agreed to swallow the poison and intoxicants — drugs and poisons, to save humanity from total extinction. Shiva then thought that every thing has some good use so the poisonous items could also be converted for the good of humanity. Thus instead of digesting the deadly poisons, He locked them up in His throat and to keep himself immune from heat and other ill effects of drugs He took the mighty Gangā (river) on His head and wrapped snakes around His arms. Thus humanity got an opportunity to benefit from poisons also by beneficence.

This mighty kindness of God Shiva was acknowledged and praised by Rishis who proclaimed that while offering obeisance to God Shiva the devotees must say ''om namah: shivāya'' — I bow down to Shiva. To make this Mantra more potent, Rishis ordained to sing: ''om namah shivāye om shivāye namah om;'' This chant became a composite obeisance for Shiva and Parvati. Normally speaking, for all other Gods, obeisance is offered by first uttering the name of the God to be propitiated such as Shree Ganeshyāya Namah or Shree Rāmaya Namah etc.

The most affable age is that of a child upto 24 months, when the child remains innocent, lying in the cradle, keeps playing and smiling, quite unconcerned with the complexities of the world. Every body loves to fondle such innocent darlings; his appearance makes the viewer cheerful. Thus in God's creations, everything is there to add to the happiness and contentment; It is only the vicious minds that interpret them perversely. Without the union of two halves you cannot have one whole. The Gods of Digamber sect of Jains and their followers remain naked; and a prominent sect amongst Hindu sadhus, called Naga Sadhus also move about naked. There is nothing obscene about it for those who have pure mind and self-control;

Such a state of living is most powerful indicator of total control over passion or pleasures of the flesh. Male and female forms are at the root of all creations on earth. When one thinks about progeny, an image of the Matru Yoni or female organ appears, but enlightened souls keep meditating on unity with the creator, that they meditate on Braham-Yoni i.e. the Kundalini which rises from under the spinal cord and travels upwards to Sahasrār (Thalamus). For those who perform Havan — sacrificial fire, for them also two essential requisites are (1) a Havan pot; and (2) to arrange the ingredients for the fire which potentiates the obeisance of deity. The psychologists call it willpower. Without interplay of positive and negative, energy generation does not occur.

Scientifically speaking, when electrons and protons come closer a momentary rubbing occurs, generating a circling motion and multiplications of atoms takes place. This coming closer generates ecstasy and sound representing Mugdh-Nritya — The blissful dance of Shiva takes place. To demonstrate, how a person can live celebate, He destroyed cupid — Kamdev, the God of passion; Later, when the other Gods appealed to Him to save and to propagate progeny He blessed Kamdev to regain his powers and energy for worldly parsons, but for himself He kept the 'bull' seated quietly in front of Himself. Thus, He is the first God to propound the harmony and superiority of having only one loving wife and two children — ideal family planning.

The renowned physicist, Murray Gelman had discovered that the basic building blocks of matter are a dozen; Six quarks and six leptons; There are anti particles, one for each of these. Particles and anti particles annihilate each other when they meet, creating a burst of energy. The six quarks are called Up, Down, Strange, Charm, Bottom and Top. Albert Einstein's famous equation, equating energy with mass, comes into play here. The shape of an atomic reactor resembles the Pindi of Shiva wherein incalculable energy can be stored for peaceful or destructive purposes. Thus, the main thing is energy — Shakti or potency which cannot be defined/described in language. No one has seen electricity, yet all of us use a bulb giving light or a fan or heavy moving machines but the basic element — electricity-remains unseen.

* * *

RUDRA NATRĀJ SHIVA

Rishis saw that instead of becoming holier and more spiritual, persons living in society were becoming increasingly vicious and avaricious. Evil appeared to be more popular than wisdom. Deeper study revealed that if a person gets what he wånts then having more of the same thing becomes repugnant so, to transform man from worldly desires to spiritual attainments in blissful settings, Rishis decided to accord religious sanction and make men receptive of the true values, so they adored God Shiva. The literal meaning of word Shiva is 'well-being' or Kalyan. God Shiva was immensely pleased with the thought that by His grace the society can become righteous, pious and spiritual, so He started dancing with ecstasy. To all those who worshipped Him with full faith, He blessed them with all that they could wish for themselves. But when after receiving coveted boons men turned vile and became indulgent, He became furious and started dancing in anger to destroy evil-doors.

Seeing these facets of God Shiva, they addressed Him as Natrāj for these attributes. The ecstasy dance was called Mugdh-Nritya (absorbing dance) and fury dance was named Rudra-Tāndava (terror dance). Thus God Shiva was regarded as the originator of all dance forms — totally 108 in numbers. At Chidambaram in Tamil-Nādu (India), a temple was built exclusively dedicated to Shiva, the Natrāj. There are 108 forms of statues carved on the Gopuram

SYMBOLS OF ŚHIVA

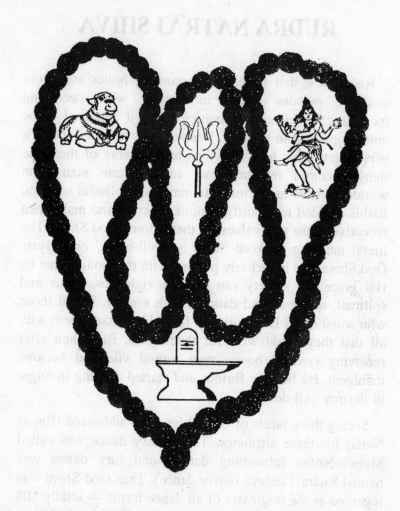

edifice — entrance gate, of this temple, depicting the Mudrās — pose, posture and expressions. The demon king Rāvan had composed a hymn called Shiva-Tāndav-Stotra, describing these postures in rousing ferver. All students of dance, start their performance/studies with prayers to Natrāj for success in their dance career.

During the rule of the CHOL dynasty kings, in the 9th century A.D., a metallic statue of Natrāj, cast in bronze, became very famous — It can be seen today in the museum at Madras (Chennai) — India. In this idol Shiva is shown standing with His right leg on the back of a demon in a dance pose. His left leg and four hands are raised and leaning towards the right side of the body; This is an extremely difficult balancing pose. His hairs are shown well-groomed, but some hairs are shown waving. On His head, the Ganga and the Moon are shown resting. In right ear He is wearing a stud and in the left a gold earring: A snake is coiled around the neck with raised hood and Shiva is wearing a garland of Rudrāksh beads. One raised left hand has a bowl of leaping flames and the other left hand is bent downwards on the right side like an elephant's trunk: He is holding a damroo — a typical music drum in his third hand and the next right hand is shown blessing the universe. He is wearing a tiger skin as a loin cloth. The idol is encased in an oval ring of flames, thus all the limbs are vibrating. in dance. This pose is called Apasmār. The uplifted leg indicates that the devotee should rise above worldly desires to attain salvation. Fire in one hand indicates purity, Shiva is performing this Tandav to the loud beat of His damroo.

* * *

SHREE LAKSMI
GODDESS OF WEALTH

All human beings cherish prosperity, health and happiness. Just as a mother alone can be very bountiful, affectionate and considerate for her children so the Rishis conceived Lakshmi as the goddess of prosperity and declared Her as the consort of Bhagwan Vishnu. The root (seed) Mantra to invoke Lakshmi is "Om shreem hreem shreem om hm̄ sa:" Her Gyatri Mantra is "Om mahālakshmī ch vidmahē vishnu patninch dhīmahi tanno lakshmi prochdayāt om". Oh Goddess Lakshmi, consort of Vishnu, I pray to thee! Oh Goddess Lakshmi, you look like brilliantly shining and appealing gold. Kindly come and be benevolent to me.

Goddess Lakshmi had surfaced after the great ocean churning along with the lotus so, Rishis seated Her on a many petalled lotus and addressed Her as Kamla; In Her praise they sang: "Oh Goddess Lakshmi, you have four hands; In one hand you are holding a lotus, in another hand you are holding nectar-pot, in the third hand you hold a conch to spread the message of righteousness and in the fourth hand you are holding a Bel-Fruit which is oval in shape representing the earth globe.

The word Shree also became synonymous with Lakshmi. This single word denotes brilliance, prosperity, grandeur etc. Persons from all walks of life covet these blessings. The king, warriors, traders, teachers, seekers, all started worshiping Lakshmi. In almost all archeological excavations in India, Goddess Lakshmi is present.

As per Skand Puran, Lakshmi had declared Her liking for religious minded disciplined, egoless, generous, gentle and benevolent persons and added that, "My abode is the home of person who is sober, pious, detached and truthful; I dislike quarrelsome, bee-minded and selfish persons; I favour industrious persons".

Shree Sukta and Lakshmi Sukta are famous hymns; They are coded formulas of chemistry for producing gold with the combination of certain herbs and a sanctified process to be performed by a Siddha saint. Such a gold brick is preserved in Indian Rashtrapati Bhawan — President House.

It is customary in India, on Diwali festival day for every devotee, to clean his residential house and office, to purify the area and offer obeisance to Lakshmi to propitiate Her. A Sanskri couplet describes that "Yashyāsti vittam sa nara kulina, sa pandita, sach shrutwan gunagya, sach priyam, sach darshaniya, sarve gunā kānchan mashra yanti". A person who commands riches, is a noble soul, he is wise man, his biddings and commands are carefully heard and respected by all; He is the darling of all; He is charming, lucky and successful person; thus all virtues are embodied in wealth".

* * *

SARASWATI GODDESS OF LEARNING

Goddess Saraswati is shining like a pearl, like the Kund Flower, like the full moon or dew drops. Her dress is pure white; She holds a Veena (musical instrument) like a royal sceptre — a symbol of authority, is seated on a white lotus. For creation, preservation and destruction; Gods Brahama, Vishnu and Mahesh worship her for deep-cool-balanced thoughts; for appropriate inspiration; Oh Devi! remove my ignorance and protect me".

In this world, wealth and knowledge — both are essential for development, growth and progress; absence of either of them can make life miserable and meaningless because Saraswati is the goddess of speech without which we can neither speak, express thoughts or undertake research etc.; Nor can we sing and praise GODS and elevated souls. Thus Saraswati is the first goddess, then Lakshmi to denote progress and prosperity to possess and enjoy the riches in life; To protect and preserve the earnings, the Rishis invoked goddess Durga -- goddess of power, Mahakali and others. After enjoying life in the world men desired salvation so Rishi again remembered to sing hymns and recited prayers to pay homage to the Gods. Thus, from beginning upto the end, everyone seeks blessings of Saraswati for all round progress and protection.

Goddess Saraswati wears bright white robes; Her vehicle — the swan is also spotless white. These attributes indicate

Satogun (truthfulness) which is the highest virtue in life. The devotee must also have a sparkling, clean character and a magnetic personality. Every single pearl is attractive and eye-catching but if the pearls get threaded together they form a necklace. Every intelligent, wise man is like a shining bulb of light, but by coming together such individuals make a girdle or a necklace.

While starting to learn, every student begins with prayers to Saraswati. Thus, all alphabets and consonants are miniature Saraswati. A child learns from the behaviour and talk of elders so the parent and teacher can create correct impression and build the character and career of the child only when their own character and career remains spotless, and magnetic. It sounds strange and astonishing that the 7 vibgyor colours of a rainbow turn white when mixed properly.

Saraswati is adi-pravartaka-introducer of all arts and skills. She is all music and gaiety. Even to punish the waywards, she uses Veena as her sceptre of authority -- she holds no weapons. Only a loving and affectionate mother can be so sweet and inspiring to enthuse the devotee.

A learned man never hankers after money; Wealthy persons find pleasures in lavish living which makes them vulnerable to down fall, whereas a wise person finds joy and happiness in nature, reading and writing about his blissful experiences. The wealth of knowledge cannot be stolen by any thief; The king cannot take it away by taxation; It cannot be divided between brothers; Truth is that knowledge increases by giving it to a genuine seeker, thus real supreme wealth is knowledge. This explains why a king is respected in his kingdom only whereas a wise man commands respect every where.

Saraswati is also the Goddess of all arts, crafts, skills, and excellence which are always joyous and colourful. Amongst birds, the peacock is the most majestic and colourful of birds full of mirth and dance so the Rishis preferred a peacock as Her vehicle. Jains also worship Saraswati; and address Her as Chakreshwari, or ShrutDevi, or Vidyawati and so on. They have a swan as Her vehicle, as also a peacock.

To remain protected by Saraswati, Shree Ramchandra as well as Shree Krishna placed Her on their head symbolically by keeping a peacock feather in their crown. Shree Lakshman had tucked a peacock feather in the head-gear of Rāma when he was preparing to proceed to participate in Dhanusha-Yagnya in the court of King Janak. Around that moment princess Sitā arrived in the royal garden to worship her deity. Shree Rama was fascinated by seeing Sita and she was also attracted towards him. Similarly, ShreeKrishna had to face all sorts of difficult and tricky situations all through his life so, from early childhood he kept a peacock feather on his head like a crown, indicating that Saraswati shall always guide and give best suited counsel, appropriate for the occasion:

"suplichh guchh mastakam devim vachmanayant deva"

Saraswati does not wear ornaments on her body; She wears a garland of fragrant flowers, all white. She holds a book in one hand, a lotus in another, a rosary in the third and a Veena in the fourth. All these symbols indicate that for looking attractive and impressive one does not need artificial decorations. Learning, sweet music and recitation of hymns are real, supreme attributes.

In Isavasopanishad, the Rishi has said that there is no end to knowledge. Those who claim to know everything, really know very little because no one can be the master of all knowledge and all the arts, and skills; One might specialise in some calling, but there also he has to admit — "Thus far and no further..." Rishis admitted the same thing by saying, — Neti...Neti; That there is no end to learning, every step we take in life has fulfillment for its goal, the urge for wholeness for its motive. It is one thing to have a philosophy and quite a different thing to live it and express it in life, character and conduct. The ass carrying its load of sandal wood known only the weight and not the value of his load; Or the spoon does not know the taste of the soup; True culture is comprehension and compassion.

Hindus as well as Sufi Saints keep a broom -- a bunch of tied peacock feathers to bless the devotee; These feathers are said to be rapid conductors of energy currents so, the aura, energy of saints can pass to the devotee by way of touching the devotee with a feather broom.

* * *

LORD GANESH
Giver of Every Success & Prosperity

"Shree Ganeshaya namh: Ganesh Poojmēdyāstu Vighnastasya nā jayatē! Aik Dantāya vidamahe, vakra tundāya dhĩmahĩ, tanno danti prachodayāt!!"

Rishi says, worship God Ganesh and no difficulties shall arise. Start all religious ceremonies and auspicious celebrations with the worship of Ganesh to avert possible mishaps. He is the commander of all regimes and giver of all success, prosperity and happiness!

The most affable and popular God is Ganesh. He is the friend and supporter of all human endeavour — a true remover of all obstacles to success; He is omnipresent in myths, legends, arts, rituals, virtues, crafts and history; Idols and statues of carvings of Ganesh have been found all over the world. It is said that Ganesh is an ideal combination of all the good and powerful elements, so He is invoked, propitiated and worshipped at the start of every auspicious function or ceremony. His followers and worshippers release and consign Him on Anant-Chaturdashi day, around August every year, and pray with zeal for his rise and return for the benefit of mankind.

Gods have many names, the count goes upto 1000. Each name indicates His appearance, shape, form, attributes, function, insignia, temperament, etc., depending upon the need of the event, occasion or solemnisation. The Rishis have fixed certain root letters to invoke every God. "gam" is the root or seed mantra for invoking Ganesh. Everyone prays to God with some objective in mind and this desire determines the manner of utterance and pronunciation. Correct sound creates positive vibrations in the atmosphere which assumes a shape representing the desired thought. Thus the shape, form and vision of God in the cosmos depends upon the quality of the devotee's call — sober, merciful, angry, etc. A good devotee sees the God in a shape coinciding with his thoughts and urges, and prays intensely for achieving success. God Ganesh is All in One. May He bless all with the fulfillment of cherished good desires.

"Shubh kāryeshu sarvadā !

The Rishis conceived of a God having all the possible virtues and attributes, so, in their vision, the form of Ganesh emerged with an elephant head to indicate that the commander must be able to think deeply and remain cool, anticipate, determine and decide about every event. So, such a God should have a large head to think deeply, undisturbed. The dog's bark does not disturb an elephant; Nor does an elephant run like a dog for food. The truth is that the Mahavat (Driver of elephants) has to coax them to have a hearty meal, otherwise the elephant refuses to eat anything. Farmers use a winnowing basket to segregate and blow out chaff or useless grains. The elephant has large ears to hear every thing but it remains unruffled and retains only whatever is valuable. Despite its large head and ears, the elephant has disproportionately small eyes. It is not the size that matters. One must have X-ray eyes to see the minutest object. The elephant can see a small needle on the ground and pick it up with its trunk. God Ganesh sees every happening.

Once, all the Gods assembled to appoint their commander. There was no consensus so they requested God Shiva to decide the issue. Shiva said that whoever completes three rounds of the earth first shall be the commander, All the Gods picked up their vehicles and the race started, but Ganesh remained seated by the side of his parents After a while, he got up, took three rounds of his parents, touched their feet and sat down. On their return, all the Gods saw Ganesh sitting merrily, so they jeered saying, "Poor chap, how could he join the race sitting on a tiny mouse?" They solicited Shiva's verdict. Shiva asked Ganesh if he had anything to say in his defence? Ganesh replied that parents represent the universe; he had completed three rounds of his parents, thus he had completed the race long age. Shiva and all the Gods appreciated his wisdom and foresight and Ganesh was accepted as the leader and was accorded first position for worship at all occasions.

Ganesh has two teeth but one is half broken denoting that everyone must have faith in one God. Knowledge can be limited, but faith must be implicit. Thus, the two teeth emphasise the difference between knowledge and faith.

Ganesh has four hands. In one hand he holds on anchor goad which keeps the elephant under control. Keeps the passions under check; In the second hand, he holds a whip with a noose — readiness to whip the unjust and unfair. In the third hand he has a bowl full of sweets indicative of total happiness, and the fourth hand is raised for blessing the faithful devotees.

Ganesh chose a mouse as his vehicle. The vehicles of the other Gods can carry them only upto the gate, whereas the mouse can take Ganesh to every nook and corner of the dwelling. With its sharp teeth and claws it can burrow any mountain. It can also swim with its claws. Thus Ganesh enjoys entry every where.

Ganesh has large pot belly which indicates that he can stomach any talk and information and use it discreetly. It also denotes that Ganesh can eat and digest any vegetarian food and remain strong and vigourous.

Rishi Vyas desired to write the Mahabharat epic and complete the book with great speed. No one came forward to accept the assignment. Eventually, Ganesh was persuaded to take up the challenge and He agreed to under-take the job on condition that the dictation must be non-stop. Rishi Vyas accepted the condition saying that "Ganesh shall not write or take down any sentence/verse without understanding its full meaning". Ganesh consented. So, whenever Rishi Vyas desired a break, he uttered a difficult verse (shlok) and Ganesh was left alone to ponder over its correct meaning before writing it. What smart mutual understanding!

* * *

NĀG DEVTĀ

God lives in the heart of all living beings. This sentence emphasises the good and evil being of all living souls not only of the humanity, but also of Animals, birds, reptiles, rodents, insects and many others species, who have contributed to human development, progress and evolution. Rishis preached respect and love for flora and fauna and for all those who have been useful in one way or the other. Snakes protect the crop from damage by rodents, and beasts. Snakes are great lovers of good fragrance and aroma. They love to be closest to sandal, kevada, ketaki and such other fragrant trees so Rishis concluded that one who loves pure scent can never be evil by nature. Some varieties of snakes thrive on pure air only — they eat nothing. This virtue indicates that one can attain the highest stage without any attachment or lust. Snakes do not bite or harm anyone until they are hurt or disturbed. The snakes eyes are said to be photogenic so after seeing any person once, it can spot that person anytime, anywhere.

Kundalini is said to be an omnipotent coiled serpent resting below the last vertibrae of the spinal cord. Lord

Shiva mastered Kundalini and accepted snakes as ornaments on His body: Lord Ganesh also adopted them as an ornament. Bhagwan ShreeKrishna had also mastered Kundalini so he could dance on the hoods of Kaliāg Nāg and drove it away from the river Jamunā to the ocean. Lord Vishnu mastered Kundalini and made Seshnāg's Its coiled body as His cosy bed; Seshnāg is said to be holding the earth on its 1000 hoods.

Gods had deputed Sursā -- the Mother of snakes to test the skill and intelligence of Hanumān just when Hanumān was readying to cross the great ocean to reach Lankā in search of Sitā;

Takshak, the king of snakes caused the death of the Great King Parikshita; Bhagwan Buddha and Bhagwan Mahavir of the Jains were protected by mighty snakes during their transcendental meditations — Tapasyā. In all the Pagodas snakes are portrayed as deities with 5 to 7 hoods. It is said that if any person is protected even from the vagaries of weather by a snake by its spread out hood, that person becomes a great king or a great saint; Hindu Tantriks believe that snakes are the Nature's or Divine guards of the treasures hidden under ground; Forest guards vouchsafe that the snake is the most reliable body-guard in the forests when their master is asleep. However, Muslims regard snakes as their worst enemies, and kill them;

In Yajurveda and Atharva veda snakes are mentioned as being, the deity of water and denoters of underground biomagnetic energy currents; They crawl zigzag while creeping on ground but when in water, they renounce all curves/twists and keep swimming like a stick — straight. Rishis reckoned that the snakes represent Kaal or Period.

The age or life span of snakes has remained undetermined to-date. King Cobra is said to be the longest and most deadly poisonous snake. In Shakun-Shastra snakes are regarded as vital/certain indicators of good or bad omen. If a snake crosses the path from the left to the right side, it brings good-luck. If a snake crosses one's path often, while on a journey by road, it indicates that some ancestor is reminding that person to perform certain religious rites for the concerned ancestor's Moksha — salvation.

Water borne snakes are not poisonous; Only some varieties of surface living snakes are poisonous, rest are harmless. In ancient times the strength of a person used to be denoted as so much snake power as opposed to modern practice of reckoning it by so much horse-power. Hindu scriptures praise snakes as rulers of Nag-Lok. Vasuki Nag is said to be their king emperor.

In Sri Lanka, Cambodia and some neighbouring countries, and Egypt, idols of snakes have been unearthed in archeological excavations. The world famous Haffkins Institute of Bombay (India) is renowned for its snake farm and laboratory where the snake poison is drawn for certain life saving drugs/preparations, vaccines etc.

In Hindu scriptures a snake king is supposed to have a saphire in its hood. The snakes cast away their upper-skin cover after a certain age, with absolute ease.

In old days, the Hindu kings used to train and nurture young attractive women who used to be fed on snake's poison; These charming ladies used to be deputed for enticing enemies or for spying on them, They were called Nag-Kanyas. Putnā the sister of king Kansa had painted her nipples with deadly snake poison in her attempt to murder infant Shree Krishna.

Nāg-Panchami day, once in every calendar year, is fixed for the feeding and worship of snakes throughout India. The snake charmers of India are known all over the world for their expertise in catching and training them; some expert Tāntriks in India and Africa eliminate snake poison using mantras and Pujā. They consider this feat as the greatest pious act that enables them to save a life.

* * *

VRIKSHA DEVTA KALP VRIKSHA

 "From times immemorial, man has lived with trees because they provided him with shelter, fuel, implements for agriculture, timber for house construction and warfare; leaves, fruits and seeds; and inspiration for spiritual growth.

Rishis endeavoured to explain spiritual truths by associating with vibrant symbols enabling the common man to see and experience those sublime truths and thus these symbols acquired religious authenticity and served allegorical purposes. Thus Rishis realised that trees are the best friends of mankind; the roots helped the conservation of soil, provided shelter to earth worms to thrive and thus increase the soil fertility; the branches and leaves were inexhaustible reservoir of oxygen — Pran-Vāyu for survival so they announced in Agni Puran — "He who plants a tree and protects it like his son, will always be remembered/respected; May the trees be the givers of peace and prosperity."

Rishis had studied total flora and fauna. They discovered that even grass has several varieties, beneficial as well as harmful; Durva grass always remains green and fresh; Kush grass has a strong fibrous structure to remain unaffected by water etc. Thus, even the grass blades were sanctified and declared as essential ingredients of worship on all ceremonial occasions.

In Rigveda and Atharvaveda some trees are deified as Vriksha Devta. Hindus consider all trees sacred and worship them for instance. Pipal (Aswattha), Banyan, Goolar, Amla, Vilva (Bel), Sandal, Neem, Mango, Babool (Acacia) are all worshipped. In ancient India, grooves of trees and flower gardens were reared with loving care. None of the sacred trees was permitted to be cut. Immortal Rishis like Valmiki, Chyavan, Dhanvantri, Bhardawaj, Charak, and Sushruta and poets like Kalidas have written volumes on trees, flowers creepers and other plants. Tulsi, Pipal, Banyan, Amla goolar, Bel and coconut were given the mythological name — KalpVriksha because these seven varieties were considered to be wish-fulfilling, and obtained from ocean churning. Some other trees are also mentioned with praise and adoration — Ashok, Kadamb, Champak, Vakul, Nagkesar, Parijat, Jamun etc. But the Banyan and Pipal acquired greatest distinction; Tulsi — a bushy plant became a must in the worship of all deities; Pipal and Banyan trees were called Bodhi-Vriksha because Lord Shiva used to sit under a banyan tree for religious discourses; and Bhagwan Buddha attained enlightenment under a Pipal tree. Even though all trees are sacred, in this chapter we are dealing with two main varieties of trees, which became associated with religion and became cultural symbols.

BODHI VRIKSHA

In Gita, Lord Krishna said, "Amongst trees I am

Aswattha — Pipal. It is said that Gods and the souls of pious ancestors rest on the branches of Pipal. A person with a strong mind and intellect alone can perform Sadhana (meditation) sitting under Aswattha because it exudes powerful energy currents with the rustling of its shiny, conic leaves to evoke inspiration and intuition. This explains why Pipal is not a Domestic tree; It is usually grown in temples or rest houses and inns, where people can come for worship. The religious sect of Visnois ceremoniously plant trees and they are always prepared to lay down their life to protect a tree instead of permitting it to be cut by anybody.

Scientists have established that in the human body, the pineal gland's secretions help the brain to remain alert and alive. The chemical properties of this secretion which stimulates understanding and intellect are found in abundance in pipal juice, hence it is called BodhiVriksha. It is interesting to note that the same chemical is present in the herbs Shankh-Pushpi and Brahammi; as also in banana and plum fruits.

In the 7th century, Huentsang — a Chinese Buddhist monk had come to India to pay obeisance to BodhiVriksha located in Gaya (India), a holy city. He was astonished to note that the leaves of BodhiVriksha had no defoliation even in autumn or summer. The leaves of BodhiVriksha wither and fall only on Buddha's Nirvan (salvation) day called Buddha Purnima and new leaves sprout the very next day, so hundreds of Buddhist and seekers assemble under this tree on that auspicious day and while returning, they take a few withered leaves with them as mementos. Emperor Ashok the Great had got a brick enclosure built to protect this BodhiVriksha.

History records that Prince Siddharth did penance and transcendental meditation in Gaya. Due to intensive Tapasya, performed without food or water for several days, he had become very weak. This made him realise that starving the body of nutrition was not correct penance; instead, one should starve his/her passions to purify the body and mind; but by then, he had become too weak even to stand on his legs. Some how he crawled upto the bank of the river Niranjana, which was flowing nearby; He took a bath, but could not muster enough strength to return to his — meditation site. Luckily, Princess Sujata happened to pass that way and noticed that a mendicant was struggling to reach the shade of Pipal tree standing nearby. She rushed to her palace and returned with a bowl full of Kheer — a delicious dish prepared with rice boiled and cooked in milk with added sugar. The Princess offered that bowl to Siddharth who ate the Kheer and felt revived and fresh. Thus on that auspicious day, under that Pipal tree, around 3.30 am — called Brahama Muhurta by the Rishis, Siddharth experienced a beaming light in his heart and mind and, thereafter he was called Gautama Buddha. It was the full moon day of Vaisākh month — May.

Intuitionally, Gautama discovered that:

1. Life in this world is a continual struggle; but

2. Ultimately salvation can be attained with a determined effort and an inner urge for real happiness; and

3. Detachment from worldly desires is the only path to remain immune from misery or wants of the body.

Gautam Buddha decided to spread these truths and propagated them for the enlightenment of all.

Thus, this BodhiVriksha became a symbol of Buddhism. Later the princess SanghMitra, daughter of King Ashoka, took a branch of this tree to Sri Lanka and planted it at Anuradhapur to commemorate and to spread the teachings of Bhagwan Buddha for attaining salvation.

In the 15th chapter of Gita, ShreeKrishna told Arjuna — "Among trees I am Aswattha." In Sanskrit, this word means that which is not today as it was yesterday. This word refers to worldly existence. Aswattha also means Pipal tree which belongs to Banyan family. The speciality of both these trees is that they supply sap from above and send it down to earth. In this respect, the functioning of the world resembles that of these trees. Both receive their sustenance from above and reach down to earthly existence. That life is self-expressive; This truth is made known to us by the leaves of the tree. He who reads and understands the Vedas is basically initiated into the study of spiritualism. Prakriti or Nature is the immortal teacher or Mother of all Truths.

Rishi Valmiki had written that Lord Shiva used to give discourses on RamCharit Mānasa sitting under the shade of a Banyan tree and this tradition was continued by Kākbhushundi who imparted the same knowledge to Garud. Folklore has it that Savitri sat under a Banyan tree and with her transcendental meditation and the power of her Satitava she drove away the Yamarāja — Lord of death who had come there to take away the life of Savitri's husband — Satyavāna. Married Hindu ladies worship the Banyan tree for a long and happy married life on the Vatsāvitri Day.

As stated earlier, Kalp-Vriksha was also obtained from ocean churning and it was gifted to Lord Indra for safe preservation because in those days it was the only known wish-fulfilling tree.

Another famous tree is called Ashok. During her captivity, Rāvan had permitted Sitā to sit under the Ashoka tree, known to relieve persons of all their worries in due course.

Yet another tree, worshiped by Hindus is the Kadam — a tree under the shade of which ShreeKrishna used to sit, play and swing.

The Amla tree was patronised by Rishi Chyavan for rejuvination properties; Vilva tree is patronised by Lord Shiva; It is the only tree which has three leaves sprouting together like a trident. It is said that the juice of its leaves provides relief to diabetics; Its fruit and the pulp within, called Bel, are the favourites of Lord Shiva. The Vaidyas prescribe eating its raw or dried pulp to stop diarrhoea. The juice of its leaves keeps sugar in blood, under control.

Almost all wellknown trees were studied for their beneficial properties; Rishis had prescribed different trees for their predominant virtues, individually as well as in combination with some other equally beneficial tree or a creeper or medicinal bushes.

* * *

TULSI

"tulsi kānanam chaiva grahē yasyāvatishthate tad grham teerth bhoot hi jāyante yama kinkarā."

Wherever Tulsi is planted, in grooves or in house-holds, that place becomes sanctified as a place of pilgrimage and the sepoys of the LORD of DEATH — Yamdoots dare not enter that place.

Lord Vishnu is perpetually shown associated with the Goddess Lakshmi and Tulsi, hence Tulsi is worshipped by all. In India it is regarded as a most sacred plant. It is a much branched erect bushy plant of about 4 ft. height. Its leaves are aromatic and are dotted with minute glands; The flowers are purplish, in small clusters on slender

spikes and the seeds are yellowish or reddish. Two varieties — Shyam (blackish) and the green are grown in houses, gardens and temples. Scientists have declared that wherever Tulsi is grown in great numbers, that area becomes pollution free. Even dried leaves retain their original properties.

The oil obtained from the leaves has the property of destroying bacteria and insects. The leaves have traces of mercury so the extract is now used as an ingredient of cancer-cure Āyurvedic medicines. The juice or infusion of the leaves is very useful in curing bronchitis, catarrh and digestive complaints; Its paste is a sure cure for ring-worm if applied regularly as also for many other skin diseases; The juice drops cure ear-ache; its decoction cures common cold; and the seeds are useful in urinary problems; it also relieves malarial fever.

Thick branch of Tulsi, when dried, is cut into beads of equal shape/size to make rosary beads for the devotees; A mala or neckless is also prepared with beads and devotees wear it with faith.

Rishis had ordained that if a ghee-lamp or incence sticks or even flowers are not available for performing Puja or worship, tulsi leaves can be offered to the deity; This explains the importance and value of Tulsi, which is even otherwise a MUST for every solemn puja or celebration.

* * *

KALASH GHAT (POT)

Rishis knew that the lightning strikes a deadly blow so, in order to escape the calamity, they developed the use of copper rods and pots, but to their dismay, they found that copper becomes blackish due to moss or fungus growth so, they enamelled or plated the pot with gold to remain bright and visible from a long distance, and placed it on the temple pinnacle.

"bhrātāh: kanchan lep goshitā vahistamrakrate sarvato ma bheshi kalsha: sthiro bhava chir devalayoshyo pari:"

All good persons, do not like to get tainted so, in order to humour the copper pot the Rishi sang above verse, "Oh brother Kalash (copper pot) do not get upset due to your gold plating by us; we promise to enthrone you for good on top of the temple so that all devotees shall know your importance and bow to your brilliance."

In early stages of civilisation men found that the rains were very helpful for crops and also provided pure drinking water but alas, rains last for a short period only during the year; They also noticed that during rains the tanks overflow and the rivers swell, causing floods, but they dry up in summer. They needed water all the year round to quench their thirst, so they developed a container — a kalash and Rishis were overjoyed to see that they could enshrine GOD Varun in the kalash and thus the worship of Varun started by worshiping the kalash; the Rishis ordained that every ceremony should start with the worship of kalash and sang in praise of kalash:

"kalsashya mukhe vishnu, kanthe rudra samāsrita: moole tatra sthito Brahma madhey matra ganā smaratah:"

"At the mouth you are Vishnu, at your throat lives Lord Shiva. Lord Brahma adores the base and at the belly all Goddesses are established, thus in a small pot, Rishis conceived the presence of all gods and goddesses and composed this hymn in their praise.

On all ceremonial occasions, a pot is filled with clean water, on the mouth of the pot fresh leaves of mango, betel-leaf etc. are kept and then a coconut is placed on top. Thereafter the kalash is decorated with Swastik and other ornamentations.

Rishis likened the human body to a kalash, saying that just as a pot contains fresh water for all occasions, the human body has the Lord within, provided the persons keep their body pure and healthy. In Hindu homes, virgin maids stand with a water filled Kalash on their head at the entrance to welcome VIPs.

• Saint Gnyaneshwar, in his commentary of Gita, called the 18th concluding chapter as kalashodhyāya. In folklore villagers sing that no one should demolish his pot simply on seeing water- bearing clouds. Such is the all pervading importance/glory of KALASH.

* * *

LOTUS

The Lotus is a very important symbol of our cultural heritage. Hindu scriptures are replete with praise of the lotus, because it is very sacred to all the GODS. "He who acts abandoning attachment, dedicating the deeds to BRAHAM, is untainted by sin like a lotus leaf by water."

God Brahama and Bhagwan Buddha are both depicted sitting on a lotus. The SUN is like a red lotus rising from the blue ocean/sky. Lord Vishnu holds a lotus in one of HIS left hands. Goddess Lakshmi also holds a lotus, presumably because both were obtained from the ocean churning. It is a water-borne flower, yet not even a drop of water stays on the lotus or its leaf, so it is regarded as the most appropriate symbol of detachment from surroundings. Poets use the lotus as a simile in praise of the feet of Gods and Goddesses. King Bharthari had composed a couplet saying, "Surrounding waters add to the grandeur of a lake with the presence of the lotus which is so beautiful and graceful — made for each other." The female lotus is called Kamalini. From SUNrise, the lotus keeps facing the SUN, and at SUNset, the lotus closes itself to blossom again the next morning. A YOGI also keeps meditating for enlightenment from morning till sunset and then retires. All the Vedas sing praises of the lotus.

In the Yoga-Shastra, the 6 Chakras are depicted with the lotus as the base. In the human body, life and strength are said to be flowing from head to toe, but in spiritual reckoning, the Kundalini rises from under the spinal cord and travels upwards, crossing lotus-based chakras to reach SAHASRĀR.

According to the Mahayan sect of Buddhism, all souls originate from the lotus. The Tibetan Buddhists and the Tantriks of Nepal recite — AUM MANI-PADMEHUM in praise of GOD. 'aum manipadme hum'.

In Muslim architecture, the lotus has no importance, but in India, the Muslim rulers used the lotus in their architecture. The Taj Mahal was built by architects and craftsmen from Arab lands, yet the architecture of the Taj Mahal remarkably differs from accepted Islamic norms. It reveals the perceptible influence of Hindu spiritual architecture. The dome of the Taj Mahal resembles an upside-down closed lotus, resting on its petals. This reveals that Shahjehan had great understanding and admiration for Yogic Chakras.

After the lotus blooms it remains fresh on its stalk for a long time, but every evening, as the Sun goes down it closes and droops. Again with the rising of Sun the next morning, it straightens up and gradually manifests full bloom and beauty again so, the sages accepted lotus as a unique symbol of unfolding the spiritual qualities of man with advent of light within himself as a consequence of developed pranayam and Kundilini.

* * *

TILAK DOT BINDU

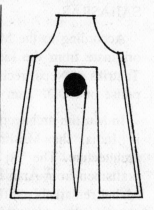

The Earliest human being saw the shape and form of his own body on earth and he also saw the burning ball like shape of SUN in the sky. This was his first acquaintance with shape. Thereafter he saw the clouds assuming incomprehensible shapes and dimensions so he decided to give shape, and form to his own ideas and thoughts and realised that the starting point of all shapes and forms is a point. Geometry recognises the point a shape without dimensions which cannot be described, still it exists. Every drawn line is a starting string of points so he conceived a starting point to describe his thoughts, visions and emotions and to express them with the help of his own sound. Thus sound and point became inter-twined. A dot or point is the seed of language expressed by sound so it was the finale of the highest attainment.

"bijākshram param bindum nādam tasyo paristhitam sa shabde sākshre kshîne ni: shabdam paramam. Shiva Shakti Niketanam Vishnu Shakti Niketanam."

A dot or point is the abode of Shiva-Shakti, Vishnu-Lakshmi-Shakti. Every person belonging to any society or civilisation had indomitable will and urge to communicate his thoughts, emotions and experiences to indicate their distinct identity, so symbols were developed.

To face the hardships and struggles of life all human beings devoted themselves to find comforts and happiness, culminating in SAT- CHIT-ANAND — truth-mind-bliss, and to establish and spread these sublime experiences, symbols and signs were evolved for faithfull depiction like — "call a rag a flag and people will rise as one entity to defend it." similarly groups of men and women adopted different types of Tilak or linear symbols which were further segregated for man/woman to wear on their body to denote their sect and idealogy.

A deep study of human anatomy revealed common, significant, exposed portions/parts of the body for applying Tilak or Bindi on the forehead and forearms. Rishis declared that the junction of the nose-root and the meeting point of the eye-brows is the most sensitive part of the body. It is the Agya-Chakra, Wheel of wisdom, and it is located there so this vulnerable spot must be kept warm and protected.

Later, Rishi Charak and Rishi Sushruta elaborated that the fore- head and forearms and temples can be used beneficially for Tilak or Bindi which can indicate as also be decorative. The most popular forms are a dot, or 'U' shape or a trident shape or 3 horizontal lines with a dot at the center called Tripund on the forehead and forearms.

Wearers of these symbols were advised to use Gorochan — a composition of lime, vermillion, turmeric, saffron, sandal, musk, agar, sindur (red oxide like powder), ash etc. for men; Women were to use sindur or vermillion on their skull- center to provide warmth to peneal and pituitary glands located near the Thalamus.

Tilak or Tripund or Bindi (dot) were declared to be helpful for good health of the brain, eyes, ears and the nose because these applications maintain a fine pull on the veins and nerves underneath the forehead, nose-root and forearms' skin, to monitor proper and adequate flow of blood mixed with oxygen. Rishis laid great importance on Tilak at these locations for better functioning of fore-brain. The human brain has over 12 billion cells called neurons which work through an inter-related and inter-connected nervous system and activate the human organs to respond appropriately.

The scientists ascribe the activities of the adrenals to the inner brain called the Thalamus. It is believed to be the most developed part of our thinking equipment. It receives all incoming sensations, judges and coordinates these suggestions when the Thalamus is stirred. It sparks off other reactions in the main cortex and a special kind of brain-washing takes place — a technique elaborately adopted and practiced by communists, dictators etc. in recent times.

The fore-brain controls the instinctive behaviour and decision making pattern of human beings. It is a relay station. Thus, in Acupressure it is considered to be most important to keep all such active and positive points pressed/pulled and kept charged like a battery, for proper and alert functioning. Incidentally the same benefits are enjoyed by ladies by wearing ornaments on their body provided the ornaments are properly made with precious metals, in the shape, size and correct weight to suit the constitution and body built of the wearer.

* * *

SWASTIK
Symbol of all round prosperity!

"swastinā. indro vradhashrvā, swastinā pooshā vishva
vedhā: swastināstakshryo arishthanemi, swastino
brahaspatir dadhātu:"

May God Indra be benevolent and kind to us: Poosha Deva — God of intelligence be pleased and be benevolent to us; Bhagwan Garud whose arms and weapons are invincible, protect us from all ills; and Bhagwan Brahaspati (Guru of all gods) protect us from all odds. Thus in this Mantra, the word 'SWASTIK' is repeated four times to ensure all blessings.

For success in every undertaking human beings pray to GOD by invoking hymns, singing praise, recitations etc. Rishis had determined a shape as a symbol to propitiate cherished desire. The root of SWASTIK is SU+US; SU means benefic and US means existence; whosoever desires to have glory prosperity, progress, success etc. is advised to invoke the SWASTIK Yantra. Aryans had adopted Swastik as a symbol for good of humanity. Hindus added some more arms to Swastik to represent happiness in married life and worldly successes. Thus, Swastik became a combined symbol for all GODS, so the traders and business community adopted it for all occasions.

Christians and the Red Cross Society and the medical fraternity adopted '+' as their symbol denoting religion, health and care of all persons. The straight verticle line represents GOD and the horizontal line denotes humanity, with full faith in GOD to traverse the world for benevolence.

Generations of research and experimentations coupled with self experience of beneficial results by Rishis, revealed that every symbol has miraculous potency. With proper usage, one can enjoy its blessings. Oriental Swastik denotes peace, prosperity and sublimation. Germans adopted the Swastik with arms extending on the left side with the argument that the angle formed by the leftward side shall move the Swastik clockwise at accelerated speed under the force of the wind. This Swastik yielded temporary temporal prosperity which ultimately resulted in ruin; The inverse or perverse use of anything will result in negativity, so Rishis ordained that the sides of Swastik arms must remain on the right side — moving or stationary for positive vibrations and benevolent results.

Dr. Antoine Bovis, a French scientist has developed a scale called the biometer to measure the energy levels surrounding men or material, a temple, church and so on. World scientists gave it the name BOVIS. Zero Bovis represents absence of all energy — death. 6500 Bovis is the energy level of a normal healthy person. 6500 to 16000

Bovis is the range of energy level of different Chakras/Yantras within the human body. The sanctum sanctorum of holy temples, churches, mosques, Gurudwaras etc. measures around 11000 Bovis. AUM has an energy level of 70000 Bovis so the chanting of AUM alone with concentration raises the physical and subtle body energy level to 70000 Bovis. The Swastik has a formidable energy level of 1 million Bovis, but in an inverse direction, the results become negative.

In book Siddhant Saagar it is written that the central point of Swastik represents the uterus the origin point of the universe. The vertical line represents Shivaling and the horizontal line represents MatraYoni — the female organ. Their cross represents formation, evolution and coming into existence of the universe. Later on the devotees added some dots also, in and around the Swastik to include all living beings in whatever shape, size or form etc they may be inhabiting the world in order that all of them may be happy and may contribute to the well being of total humanity.

Rishis believed that human beings are a miniature form of the universe. Whatever is visible on all planets is also present in a human body in a minute/abridged form so, it is within the reach of all evolved souls to awaken and utilise all pervading energies. These facts establish beyond doubt that the ancestors of men were not monkeys.

Plato who was a great thinker/seer of Greece, had put up a notice on his research lab — "NO admission for those who have no knowledge of geometry and advanced maths" because apparently abstract shapes and figures are not merely diagrams; But materialistic symbolic forms of what a devotee is contemplating and meditating upon. The triangles, squares, penta-hexa-octagonal shapes etc. represent a deity, so when a devotee propitiates and invokes that deity through the medium of selected diagrams for the fulfilment of some cherished desire or seeks a boon, his concentrated thoughts concretise and yield results. Swastik is one such omnipotent symbol. A Siddha Yogi alone can explain its all embracing significance, potency and efficacy with worship procedures.

* * *

SUDARSHAN CHAKRA

Sudarshan Chakra, Lotus, Lakshmi (Goddess of Wealth), and the conch were obtained as gifts from the great ocean churning. Lord Vishnu accepted these gifts and He keeps them close to His heart. Lord Vishnu uses Sudarshan Chakra as His invincible weapon to punish evil doers. The enigmatic aspect of Sudarshan Chakra is its unfailing capacity of chasing the target upto destruction unless it is commanded by the Lord to return without harming the target. Rishi Durvāsā had to face this ordeal when he tried a foul attempt to denigrate king Ambreesh. Rishi Durvāsā ran to save himself from attack but no one could save him from the infinite chase of Sudarshan Chakra. He was advised to approach Lord Vishnu for pardon. He surrendered himself to Lord Vishnu, but Vishnu declined to spare him until king Ambreesh agreed to pardon the Rishi so Durvāsā went to king Ambreesh, apologised for the wrong he had done to the king and the king was please to appeal to Bhagwan Vishnu to pardon the Rishi.

Bhagwan ShreeKrishna also had a Sudarshan Chakra in His right hand; He also used the Sudarshan to punish the evil doers only. King Shishupāl was hostile towards ShreeKrishna. He had told Shishupāl not to exceed beyond 100 abuses or derogatory words. In his antagonism, Shishupāl ignored this warning so ShreeKrishna beheaded him as soon as he crossed the limit.

The word Sudarshan conveys two meanings (1) Good to look at; and (2) easily visible; But the word Chakra — a circle or a wheel, makes the matter complicated because this composite word can be interpreted to mean Time; Or Day/Night, or months, or the different seasons moving in a circle. To explain, Sanskrit has two words derived from the same root — Pratimā = a statue; and Prateeka = symbol. The first word creates the shape of an image, whereas the second is purely indicative of many hidden meanings. A Chakra as a symbol reveals a deeper insight. In their obeisance to God Sun Rishis prayed.

"God Sun, seated on a chariot of wheels, glittering like gold, holding a Lotus in hand, be kind to us".

Initially this couplet was composed in praise of God Sun who looked like a red hot circle to become benign because the Rishis had realised that if Sun becomes angry He might dance in fury called Pralaya Tāndava and that shall be the end of this world. The same fear of world coming to an end is expressed in the Shiva Tāndav; in fury dance of Lord Shiva where He is shown with an aura of leaping flames around Him.

Great kings and emperors adopted the Chakra as the symbol of authority; Mighty kings used to assume the title of Chakravarti Sāmarāt (monarch of all he surveyed) and neighbouring kings had either to accept and agree to his suzerainty or be prepared to settle in battle.

The epic Mahābhārata mentions a very interesting episode. A disciple named Uttang had bought ear-rings to be presented to the wife of his Guru but a demon-Takshaka, stole them. To regain the ear-rings Uttang chased Takshaka right upto hell. In that under-world called Pātāl Lok, Uttang saw 6 princes driving a giant wheel of 360 spokes. On his return, he enquired from his Guru about the significance of that wheel. Rishi Deerghtamā declared that a giant wheel with spokes keeps moving non-stop in the cosmos. The 360 spokes represented 360 days of a year and the 6 charming princes moving the wheel incessantly are the 6 seasons of the year.

Bhagwan Buddha had also introduced a wheel for prayers, called the Dharma Chakra. Buddha said to his followers, "come, let us put our shoulder to the wheel to move". This wheel develops upto 13000 Bovis energy when rotated with speed by the followers of Buddhism as prayer rounds. This practice helps the devotees to increase their concentration/meditation.

Bhagwan ShreeKrishna had also said the same thing differently, "I have come to set in motion the power of Dharma-Righteous Duties. Quarreling and fighting is not the true nature of noble souls. Spirituality is the privilege of every individual".

Shiva tantriks had developed certain geo-mechanical devices encompassed in a wheel frame representing the cosmos. They divide the universe into a triangle representing Sat-Chit Anand — Truth-Mind-Bliss. In Kundalini awakening, the devotee arouses the 7 chakras located in the body through well defined Prānayām process.

History records that Babylonians also knew the use of the wheel.

In old Egyptian temples wheels were in use before 3000 BC.

If the bark that protects the tree fails to grow and expand along with the growth of the tree, it shall choke that tree; But if it is a living tree, it will shed and break the bark and grow new bark for itself. The age and growth of trees is also ascertained by the number of circular rings which appear on the stem every year.

The enigmatic aspect of a wheel is the axle around which the wheel moves, but the axle remains undisturbed.

Whether I call you ear-ring or anklet,
Or name you as broach or a bracelet;
The inherent gold glitters bright in You,
So is the Self, shining through in view.

* * *

SHREE CHAKRA : SHREE YANTRA

The garbh-grah — sanctum sanctorum of Lord Venkateshwarā's temple in India has a highly powerful Shreeyantra beneath the foundation, so this temple has become a Wish-fulfilling holy place for real devotees. It is the richest temple in India.

It is claimed that a ShreeYantra made with 5 metal alloys in the prescribed composition as laid down by Rishis and sanctified by a Siddha saint, acquires undisputable potency of bestowing riches on the devotee for several years as per the potency infused in it.

Sir John Woodruff and Dr. N.J. Button of U.K., and Dr. Zejerta of Germany have undertaken a deep study and research on the scientific construction and celestial effects of ShreeYantra. In Russia, Dr. Alexi Kulaicheva has attempted to analyse and study the formation of Shree Chakra or Shree Yantra on a computer to establish its precision and accuracy. Scientists in China, Japan and the spiritual heads of Tibet and Nepal have studied Shree Yantra and its cosmic effects with proper propitiation as prescribed by Rishis.

The Tantriks developed certain well defined geo-mechanical devices encompassed in a wheel representing the cosmos, saying that the whole universe is bound in a circle. They divide the universe into a triangle with an apex on top representing Sat-Chit-Anand, or Fire, Shiva and Male. They also drew triangles with a downward apex to represent Water, Energy and Nature. A combination of both such triangles, crossing the arms of each other represents Creation-Preservation-Destruction. The center point of both triangles remains unchanged representing Braham — The great Source of all creations. Jagat Guru Ādi Shankarāchārya has given a vivid description of Shree Yantra in his book Sondarya Lahari.

To propitiate Goddess Lakshmi, there are two independent collections, Shree Sukta and Lakshmi Sukta. It is said that Shree-Sukta has been written in coded language. In fact, it gives details of a chemical formula, following which gold can be made with a specified mixture and a combination of juices of certain herbs available in India.

Those who worship a Shree Yantra are advised Not to use saffron in their puja-offerings. The best and recommended offering for puja or worship is some vermilion and a natural fragrance called Itra in India. A Shree Yantra should not be worshipped or disturbed at night.

* * *

SHREE YANTRA SHREE CHAKRA

To propitiate Lakshmi — the Goddess of Wealth & Prosperity, this yantra/Chakra is worshipped as prescribed.

THE WHEEL OF SRI. SAKTAS use mantras (spells) and yantras (diagrams) in their worship. This diagram is called Srichakra: it symbolises the union of Siva and Sakti. The four triangles with apex pointing upward represent Siva, the five pointing downward depict Sakti. The bindu (also Satki) is in the smallest triangle with the apex pointing downward.

120

A Yantra is a geometrically scientific device/construction. In the spiritual process, a yantra embodies the energies and powers of its deity. In Kularnava Tantra (5.86) it is said to denote the relationship between a person's soul with body, or of oil with the wick of a lamp.

A Yantra is the radiating beam and power of its deity. The Rishis said that every human body is the miniature form of Universe consisting of all energy, power, glow or darkness in specific proportions with an in built capacity of the vibrations, sound and heat necessary for development, expansion and disintegration in space.

* * *

VASTU SHASTRA

Rishis have written and codified Vastu Shastra with, amazing details about the different dimensions of buildings, temples, forts, townships with their layout, land scaping etc. Architecture was regarded as a venerable science.

Mastering the earth and cosmic energies — garuda not permitting the serpents to cross at the feet + receiving cosmic energies by holding their tails as antennas

In ancient times, architecture was not only the building of a structure to limit or define space; It was inherently a sacred science for three dimensional constructions, erected in harmony with the laws of Creation which surround us in forms/shapes that exist in Eternity. A sacredness of proportions, materials, a mysticism of harmonies and of colours a critical choice of right location, orientation, a correct choice of the Nakshtra — hour to start construction activity etc. so that the matter and form could express in infinite was the cosmic truths; to bestow on humanity the multiple benefits of the Infinite.

Bio-electrico-magnetic grid radiations of the earth, and the radiations of under ground streams of water, faults in the earth structure/layers, cavities below the surface, and earthquake-prone regions were graphically represented by snakes and the divine bird Garud is shown as holding the snakes under each claw and not allowing the snakes to cross the indicated mastery over the earth energies.

Human beings are vitally affected by these energies at their place of work, rest, sleep, etc. because the body remains stationed in such areas for long hours. It is of utmost importance to have buildings designed and oriented in such a way that, by themselves, they also generate positive vibrations for success, prosperity and health.

To remain healthy and alert, the brain must constantly receive copious oxygen as well as suitable quality blood supply from the heat. Nature has provided blood barriers near the Medulla-Oblongata to refuse and return unsuitable blood supply even if one were to stand on his head. Magnetic polar currents flow from South Pole to the North. By facing the North, we face the direction of current which will keep passing over the head and thus help the brain to remain healthy and strong. These scientific truths explain how and where to sit for Puja, to work in the office, to sleep and rest; Of course, the moon's position in the birth chart of every individual also helps in arriving at correct decisions for above purposes.

The principles of Vastu Shastra are based on physical geography, rain-fall, isobars, winds, ocean currents, isotherms natural vegetation, climatic regions, rivers, water resources, mineral areas, density of population etc. of every nation, big or small; Its principles are scientifically accurate if the above aspects are properly understood and reckoned. Its strength is in its knowledge of the country's climate and culture. Vastu Shastra is basically the utilisation of living space so that it harmonises the person with the elements by working in harmony with earth's magnetic currents. In

India, in South-West we get a lot of Sun, so Vastu dictates that this part of the building should be a protective shield for comfortable living areas in the rest of the living quarters. On the North-Eastern side there is more shadow or mellow Sun so this part should be kept open, not necessarily vacant. To explain, in India, every race course has structures on the Western and Southern side so horses run on the North-East; Thus the South-West is closed and the North-East has remained open. One can build more floors on the Western side while keeping some open terrace on the Eastern side. Again, in North-Eastern room, try and provide doors/windows on the Eastern and North-Eastern side, preferably with a balcony or verandah and block south-western side. This precaution can ensure no heart ailment for the residents.

In India as per Vastu Shastra, North and East are more auspicious. Select the plot which may be a square, rectangular or shaped like a trapezium; Avoid a triangular plot, otherwise you risk blocking the Energy Waves. North-East is the air zone, so the transient utilisation of this space from Vastu angle is best suited for a drawing room or guest room; not the master bed-room. Master bed-room is best located in the south-west. If located in South-East, the married life will remain inflammable. But the owner can keep his working office here for better energy. The North-East or North corner can be used as a main entrance. The North-East corner is dedicated to water, so water-tanks or tube- wells can be located on this side.

The South-East side is dedicated to fire so locate the kitchen here or in the North-West. If kitchen is in the South-West side, sickness shall remain a constant risk.

Best advice is to use one's own common sense in the design and actual construction. For instance in coastal regions houses having South and West sides open will have more fresh air. In Chandigarh, India, the renowned architects have provided more windows and less walls. The windows are more rectangular like bricks dimensions and at eye-level for better circulation of air and natural light — healthier living conditions.

LEVELS OF THE PLOT ...INSIDE

The ground levels should be slightly higher in South and West. Ground levels in North & East should be lowest in the plot. Levels in South East & North West should be equal levels. North levels are better lower than the South. East levels should be lower than the West.

LEVELS OUTSIDE THE PLOT

This aspect may not be under the control of the plot owner himself so only precautionary observations are mentioned here.

East and North levels of the adjoining plot or the road should be lower.

Towards South and West mounds or raised levels are helpful.

Ponds, tanks or rivers in the North or East or North-East give good results.

A pond or tank or well or ditches towards South-West yield bad results.

A high building built towards the South or west or South-West of the plot is good for prosperity.

WELLS OR WATER RESERVOIRS

East side well/pond/tank should be towards the North. North side well etc. should be located towards the East. A well in West or South or South-West or North West or South-East is not good.

A well opposite the main entrance or opposite doors opening outside is risky. Never have a well in the middle of the building — This does not apply to wells built for throwing sweepings etc. down to the ground floors for collection of rubbish.

Feng Shui is the Chinese art of arranging buildings and their contents in a manner so harmonious with the environment that good fortune is assured or at least bad-luck is averted. Basic thought is that the motion of QI — a life giving cosmic breath usually associated with the dragons that keep lurking in natural habitats. Buildings must be so designed that QI — is encouraged to accumulate and circulate in them. As a rule, there is one main accumulation of QI near the dragon's genitals. Indian Rishis also emphasised this area as belonging to Kundalini.

* * *

RUDRAKSHA

Rudraksha is the seed (stone) of a fruit of a rare specie of a tree found in Nepal, Java, Sumatra and Malaya. In India, it has been spotted at some centers in Konkan and Karnataka. It is roundish with a cellular demarcation and has a central bore. Small or unripe, unmatrued seeds are of no value. Rarely a seed with no bore is also seen but then it becomes a piece of great sanctity value if it has only 1 cell mark. The cellular mark/division varies from 1 to 21 per seed. Rishis observed these peculiarities and made detailed investigations because they noticed that every seed is a ball of energy but the efficacy quantum differed from piece to piece with different cellular markings but there was no difference in any 2 identical seeds so, they accorded to Rudraksha a place of pride as mentioned in Rigveda, Atharwaveda, Skand Puran and other scriptures because of its beneficial properties of attracting healthy vibrations. Saints wear it as a necklace; Rishis had deified it as an ornament of Lord Shiva. Because of its varying energy potential, rare availability and sanctity accorded by Rishis, it is very much in demand, by the believers; people are willing to pay any price for a one cell Ruderaksh without a bore. Most common and easily available variety is the 5 cell mark.

Real rudraksha is solid in construction so it sinks in a bowl filled with water. A fake piece shall float. There are many other scientific tests to determine the purity/efficacy, and aroma. Its aromatic property helps a devotee to go into deep meditation early. It must be remembered that Rudrāksha must not rub against itself or even with the fingers of a devotee so its use in a rosary is forbidden because rubbing/friction can erode its potentiality and charm property. It can be worn on the neck threaded with gold/sliver wire, in a silk or woolen thread so that it remains in gentle touch with the body to boost immunity. Just as a doctor uses a stethoscope to examine a patient, enlightened saints use Rudraksh to read the personality and fortune of disciple. It determines positive or negative energy currents flowing in the body of every person at any time. The blood pressure of the wearer becomes normal. Its energy charges help and strengthen the heart, reduces tension.

According to Ayurveda, it is said to be sour and hot. It quenches thirst if milk with a minute quantity of its paste is mixed and drank. Sages advise to put 1 or 2 seeds in a sliver or copper pot or water jug and sip that water whenever thirsty to keep blood pressure under control.

A single seed retains the efficacy for about 1 month. Lightening does not strike the wearer; protects him from accidents; and bestows good luck. Persons with positive energy currents should wear on the right hand; with negative currents on left hand, for better results; persons wearing Rudrāksh are held in high esteem.

* * *

SACRED THREAD

A thick tuft of hairs on head, a rosary in hand, a prominent Tilak or Tripund on the forehead and a sacred thread across the torso are the accepted symbols of being a holy man amongst the Hindus.

To encourage cooperation and establish order in society, Hindus had divided the life span of every person into four distinct divisions — Brahmacharya — the celebate life of a student; Grihasta — family life; Vanprastha — the third portion of life when a person should detach himself from family bonds and endeavour to serve the society; and Sanyasa — when a person should finally renounce the world, In this final stage the person ceases to belong to his family, caste, or creed, Instead he devotes himself to spread the message of the scriptures of love and benevolence and simultaneously practices Yogic Sādhna to illuminate his own self to attain salvation. There is no sanction for leading an idle life and thus become a burden on society or to look to pass life in an old-age-home run with the help of others. To make life simpler and enjoyable, Lord ShreeKrishna preached secularism, saying, "I have divided mankind in 4 stages (Ashrams) as per their competence/capability and deeds (calling) or professions so, there is no need for any class conflict, or haves and have nots in society.

By birth, every child is a Shudra because they cannot clean themselves. As the child grows, it develops his/her talents. Just as a uniform is compulsory in good educational institutions, similarly, the child used to be initiated in a Gurukul (co-educational institution) run by some renowned Rishi and at that time, a sacred thread ceremony used to be performed by the Guru to denote that the boy or girl is now reborn and adopted in intellectual society.

After completing his educational career, the Brahamchari was free to join the ancestral family business and excel in it or if his talents dictated any other career then he had to prove himself worthy of the solicited switch-over. Thus, every young person had a birthright to progress in his family business without any apprehension of discrimination; and for diversion, he had to prove his worth. Exceptions to good rules exist every where; the intervening dark age period aggravated the situation and misunderstandings cropped up, giving room to class struggles for existence and survival. There was no caste system initially; the classification used to be based on the reputation of Gurukul and the reputation of the Rishi running it; The nature and requirements of any profession determined the class/calling.

Rishis did not propagate mass education because ordinarily every human being has a limited intelligence/competence/capability for excellence; Only a born genius or a person gifted with dexterity and zeal could rise above contemporaries by virtue of his/her excellence and for such persons the sky was the limit for progress upto attaining Moksh — salvation. Thus, Rishis offered an equal opportunity to all students and disciples to prove their merit without caste considerations or family.

A sacred thread consists of hand-spun yarn of specific length; Three equal lengths of yarn are twisted together to make one standard length. Thus, 3 twisted yarn lengths are tied together and after a well defined sacred thread ceremony, the student used to be initiated, to give him a sacredness status; The student was advised to wear the sacred thread like a cross belt on his body. The 3 twisted threads represented Trinity of Gods; or 3 virtues of life — Satogun (pious living), Rajogun (imperious living), and Tamogun (vicious living); The 3X3 also represented Navagrah — 9 planets recognised by astrology; as also the 9 outlets of every human being — 1 mouth, 2 nostrils, 2 eyes, 2 ears, 1 genital organ and the anus, The rishis vested the desciple with a sacred thread in order that he should constantly remember of having taken a vow to keep under check and control these 9 outlets for a healthy, long life.

The wearer of sacred thread becomes a leader because every thread blesses the wearer with increased longevity; all the threads are bright white so they add to the aura and moral strength. There can be no dispute in acquiring knowledge by deeds and single minded efforts.

Zoroastrians also wear a sacred thread as a belt around their lumbar region. Wearing a belt is recommended by medical science also to keep the lumber region vertebraes in position and proper alignment, so the military, police, security guards and others have adopted this practice. However the Rishis did not recommended wearing it around the back in order to retain its purity and sacredness — the lumbar region is considered to be unhygienic. Additionally, the wearer was told to use it for tying around the ear while attending to nature's calls. Rishi Sushrut and Rishi Charak commended this practice as a health need to keep the veins of ears and nose in alert position; and the Dhoti (loin cloth) around the back kept the lumber region

in good shape/alignment. This is better expressed and
explained in acupressure therapy.

* * *

DEEPAK JYOTI FLAME

'tamso mā jyotirgamaya'

"Lead me Oh! kindly light (flame), lead me from darkness to light! No person feels happy with living in darkness. Rishis always worshiped 'Jyoti' (flame) as being the purest of the pure because it consumes all impurities, yet it remains pure so, they worshipped fire, the lightening in the clouds, God Sun, Moon, and also the twinkling stars emitting dim light to remove the darkness. The electric bulb cannot light up another bulb so the bulb is not worshipped but a Deepak (lamp or a candle) takes pride in lighting up other Deepaks even at the cost of burning out itself. The Sun and Moon do give light but they are up above in the sky; They are constantly moving away, whereas the fire/flame remains on earth as the eternal companion of mankind.

Skand Purān says, "fire burns up every thing, whereas a lamp, and a candle destroy darkness and spreads light".

"Oh lamp, I bow to thee; You are supreme God; You are ShreeKrishna; you burn up our sins, I bow to thee!" Flame can infuse knowledge, wisdom and thus make others happy. The navigators keep on right track by seeing the beams of light-house.

Bhagwān Buddha addressed his disciples saying, "Oh enlightened souls become a lamp to spread the glow of light and thus brighten up every thing.

"Who will take up my work? asks the setting Sun". None had an answer in the whole world; An earthen lamp humbly said, 'I will, my Lord as best as I can'. As a lamp in windless place does not flicker, this is the simile used to discipline the mind of Yogi, practising concentration on God.

A lamp is a earthern saucer like container. It is filled with Ghee (butter), then a twisted cotton tape is immersed into it and the top end is lit in every Hindu home and temple. The tape keeps sucking the ghee to yield a cool bright light, a flame. Burning oil is not recommended, because it produces black smoke soot.

In nature, the flame is considered to be the source of infinite energy of positive currents. If you have an even number of flames side by side, they cancel each other's radiation and become harmful; The smallest flame of any type radiates infinite energy. This explains the value and sanctity of odd numbers of flames. Great emphasis was laid on 'ārti'in India at the time of concluding any worship or Havan. The ārti — flame is moved around the idol for devotees to have a look of deity from top to toe. Then the devotees put out their palms to receive the ārti aura; in those few seconds the body's energy level rises to that of the flame. Scientists have tried interesting applications of flame t cure certain physical ailments -- it is a germ killer.

Rishis and enlightened souls aroused the Kundalini from Her seat to rise up and illuminate all Yogic-Chakras upto Sahasrar (Thalamus). Flame and light always elevate the depressed into beaming joy!

* * *

RINGING OF BELL, SOUNDS, (GHANTĀ, DHWANI)

Centuries ago, all the children used to go to Gurukul (a Residential Institutions for total studies), situated in forests, away from townships. The killing of beasts, reptiles, birds etc. in and around the Gurukul was strictly prohibited yet all the students, teachers and residents had to be protected from beastly attacks. Besides animal attacks, all the inmates had to be protected from various diseases, infections and weather changes throughout their educational career — students returned home only after completing their studies of chosen careers.

After meticulous research and experiments the Rishis discovered that metallic sounds and strong wind currents can kill bacteria and germs and also drive away the beasts. To create effective sound with single instruments, a bell was determined to be the best device, because a bell cast with metal alloys of different metals, in specified composition of 8 different metals, made the most effective sound with resounding echo which spread in the surroundings. The composition and dimensions of metal alloys were also determined scientifically. Regular rhythmic ringing of heavy and light bells and plates which were beaten like drums was introduced and made compulsory at the time of every worship, every day, to invoke the deity's blessings for all inmates, as is done in all churches to summon the faithful for prayers.

Africans also use the bell to ring out poison of snake bite of any patient; Witch doctors do so mostly.

In 1916 the High Court of England had deputed 3 eminent scientists to ascertain the effects of bell ringing; The scientists established that with the sound of a standard bell physical and mental diseases can be cured; Rhythmic sound is pleasing to the ear. In 1928 Berlin University conducted intensive research and found that with loud sounds of the bell or the blowing of conch, upto 27 cubic feet of air gets purified in an area of 1220 sq. ft. and declared it to be the most economical way of killing bacteria to purify the surroundings. In Chicago Dr. Bryne cured 1300 patients of their deafness.

In IInd World War, Germans had produced float mines filled with a humming sound akin to that of war planes so, whenever any enemy plane flew over such mine and the two humming sounds coincided, the plane burst in mid air.

Rishis had classified the sounds in different categories for different purposes. For war like preparations the Conch, Damroo, Nagarā, Damdamā, Bheri, Turhi etc. were used during war; For appealing music Bānsuri, flute, Veenā Sārangi, Santoor etc. were used to the accompaniment of Tablā, Mridangam etc. For worship, the blowing of conch, bells of different dimensions, the beating of metallic-alloy plates, Jhānj, Majirā etc. were common.

In temples, from early morning till late night, the devotees continue to chant hymns, prayers and songs using musical instruments, in order to invoke divine blessings via different sound waves. This explains the purity and sanctity of sanctum sanctorum.

Rishis had discovered that the universe is filled with different sounds and notes so they codified each note, gave it a form and a correct, appropriate pronunciation. Sanskrit has 50 alphabets encompassing the whole universe. They sanctified each alphabet with a specific potency or energy; From 'A' to 'Ha' (Z), every letter is endowed with energy and potency; When correctly uttered and pronounced, the potency, appropriate for the occasion/situation, radiates/materialises. This can be learnt from a self-realised Siddha-Saint only. Audio tapes also recite and repeat prayers when played, but their sound does not produce any real effect because they lack the life force of human vibrations, which a Siddha-Saint alone can infuse. This explains the value attached to blessings so eagerly sought from elders/enlightened persons.

The world scientists have also proved that with sweet and melodious music, the yield of milk from bovines increases; and saplings become healthier and grow faster. Rishis could tame the tiger or the snake alike with chanting of effective prayers. Accomplished faith healers claim to cure diseases and achieve successes when they persue with full faith and concentrated meditation on fulfillment of desired objective, with the true techniques as established by Rishis; If any of these factors and appropriate pronunciation of Mantra is absent, the effort becomes futile. This is the concretisation of sounds.

* * *

WISH FULFILLING COWS

Rishis had propagated cow worship ages ago, when the word Hindu was not known. Mercy or pity for the helpless is the kindest sentiment/emotion. Cows provide health, nourishment and easily digestible milk for everyone; cow-dung is the best fertiliser and it is the best material for feeding a bio-gas-plant for generating required electricity and energy on domestic level; cows give birth to bullocks for agricultural processes + surface transport by bullock carts in return for very little care, fodder and water; cows are pure vegetarians so they never become ferocious unless they are very badly treated, but once they become furious they become belligerent and can fight a lion also in self protection, so cows alone deserve greater reverence from human beings in comparison with other animals so, Rishis advocated cow-worship as the worship of one's own mother; This respectful and kind treatment of the cow also point their compassion for all animals, even beasts. There is no other animal so very beneficial and economical for humanity.

Bhagwan ShreeKrishna treated cows and calfs as companions.

Prophet Mohammed Saheb also advocated cow worship in the Holy Quran; not cow slaughter.

Kāmdhenu was the sacred cow of Gods. Her daughter — Nandini was gifted to Rishi Vashishtha, by God Indra.

Emperor Dilip regarded it his sacred duty to tend to this cow daily because Nandini was gifted with wish fulfilling power. The other well known cow was called Kapila.

According to Ayurveda, the best and healthiest milk is obtained from a black cow; The second best , is a reddish-brown coloured skin cow; White or spotted cows are just normal cows.

* * *

CONCH SHELL SHANKH

Shankh was obtained as a gift from the great ocean-churning. The spiral formation inside the conch-shell is symbolic of infinite space which gradually expands in clock-wise direction.

 An attractive Shankh with its mouth on the right side was accepted by God Vishnu and another with a left-side opening adores the hand of Goddess Lakshmi hence both these special types are considered auspicious. The blowing of Shankh heralds every important event and auspicious celebration to call the faithfuls at the beginning of worship of the deity.

On the battle field of KuruKshetra in the Mahābhārat, every morning the start of warfare was signaled by the blowing of the Shankh and again every evening, the war for that day used to be ended with blowing the Shankh. Every great king and army-chief had his own particular Shankh. Some of the famous known Shankhs are:

PANCHJANYA	This Shankh was always used by ShreeKrishna;
DEVADATTA	was used by ARJUN;
MAHĀ SHANKH	was used by Bhimmā;
ANANT VIJAY	was used by Yudhishthir;
MANI PUSHPA	was used by Sahadeva;
SUGHOSH	was used by Nakul; and
POUNDRA	was used by Vrikodar

DIVINE MUSICAL INSTRUMENTS

Aryans had developed several musical instruments suitable for every occasion, ceremony. Some typical yet very simple, musical instruments became attributes of Gods and Goddesses.

DAMRU — A small hand drum was adopted by God Shiva;

BANSURI — A bamboo flute which became a close companion of ShreeKrishna;

VEENA — Saraswati Goddess of Learning and Fine-arts adopted Veena as her celestial musical instrument.

BHERI & TURHI etc. were used by the army in accompaniment with NAGARA & DHOL to announce war or some such uncommon event.

BINA & KARTAL — These instruments were used by Rishi Narad and later became popular with almost all saints.

* * *

BETEL LEAF
Called Pan

Preservation and propagation of flora and fauna were an essential activity of life. All trees and creepers are man's best friends. The peepal, Amlā, Banyan, Ashok, Palāsh, Goolar, Shami, Neem etc. are worshipped every where in India. The leaves of mango and Ashok are tied in a long string and hung at the entrance to welcome deities and VIP guests. During worship or rituals, leaves from select trees are used as essential accessories, but amongst all leaves, betel leaf enjoys a place of pride. In Hindu weddings a betel leaf is tucked into the head-gear of the bride and bridegroom. The use of betel leaf is considered as a noble trait; On all auspicious celebrations betel leaf and a few other leaves have become symbolic items denoting freshness and prosperity.

In Skand Purān it is written that betel leaf was obtained from ocean churning. Epic Mahābhārat narrates that after their victory, the Pandavās decided to perform Rajsuya Yagntya. The performing sages asked for betel leaves to start preparation but alas, the leaves were not available so Arjun was advised to proceed to Nāg-Lok, the kingdom of snakes in order to procure them. Arjun approached the Vāsuki Nāg queen to oblige. The queen was pleased with Arjun's appeal, cut a phalange of her little finger and gave it to Arjun and advised him to sow the phalange from which a creeper shall grow and sprout with many leaves. Since the seed of this creeper was a human phalange, this creeper is not blessed with any kind of flower of fruit. Thus pan creeper was obtained from the snake queen Vāsuki so it is called Nāg-Valli or Nāgarbel.

Pān has enjoyed political overtones also, by becoming prestigious link between two mighty civilisations. Aryans ruled North India and South was ruled by Dravids. Rishi Jamadagni had his Ashram on mount Mahendra in Utkal, ruled by Nāg kings. According to kathā Sarit-Sāgar, queen Surigāwati had taken shelter in the Ashram of sage Jamdagni. Her son, Prince Udayan saw pān leaves in the Ashram for the first time, and requested his mother to ask for a pān creeper as a souvenir. Thus Pān became prestigious because Nāg king was pleased to present the creeper to the Prince and this exchange formed a vital link between North and South. Mention of the use of betel leaf in some form or the other is available in all famous epics — Rāmāyan, Mahābhārat, as well as Buddha and jain scriptures.

Pān has rich herbal properties. In is invigorating and energising, a killer of germs/bacteria and eliminator of cough. It is astonishing that eating a fresh betel leaf is forbidden by Ayurveda on the ground that is can cause blisters on the tongue and increase acidity, whereas if it is kept in water for 1 full day and then eaten, it becomes digestive. In the book Rājvallabh, it is specifically mentioned that before eating a pan, pluck its stalk, cut the edge tip and scrap its veins because all these are injurious for human health in general and the brain in particular. In Nighntu, — the great Ayurvedic compilation by sage Dhanwantari, it is mentioned that two varieties of betel leaf can be eaten — whitish and blackish; The blackish variety

144

is said to be constipative but the whitish eliminates cough and is digestive.

* * *

COCONUT — SHRIPHAL — NARIYAL

For success and prosperity on all occasions, the beginning is done with the breaking of a sanctified coconut; small bits of kernel are distributed amongst all the assembled persons. All religions functions and rituals start with worshiping a coconut because it is regarded as the symbolic GANESH — the deity due to whose benevolence the job or performance undertaken attains its successful conclusion without any hindrance. While starting his first lesson, the student offers a coconut to the GURU — teachers, with a request to initiate teaching.

Sage Vishwāmitra is said to be the creator of this wonder fruit. When GODS pushed down king Trishanku from heaven, Vishwāmitra became furious and decided to challenge Brahmā — the creator of the universe and announced that the small will create a parallel world. He began with creating artificial summer by changing the refreshing weather around October. The sultry heat of four weeks duration is called Vishwāmitra's summer. In place of human heads, he created coconuts with two eye like sockets and a beard. While he was readying himself to infuse life in the coconuts, Lord Brahmā appeared and advised him to give up his project. Vishwāmitra agreed to give up provided the coconut was blessed with dignity and respectability. Brahamā conceded saying that all auspicious functions and celebrations shall be solemnised with the presence of coconut and added that if any pious housewife would eat the seed of a one eyed coconut, she shall be blessed with a child. Thus sage Vishwāmitra agreed to gave up his project, yet in order to endear his wonder fruit to posterity he added symbolic powers.

For every person, engaged in spiritual pursuits, the coconut symbolises crowning success. Its hard kernel inspires one to do hard work for attaining success and glory; indicates concerted effort to break the barriers of wandering thoughts and desires when its hard shell gets broken, the bliss of self realisation can be experienced like pure white and sweet kernel, and the milk of kindness flows to bless. The worldly persons gain strength and improved eye sight by eating the kernel; sick and elderly persons find its milky water nourishing. Ladies apply its oil for luxurious hair-growth with silky shine.

It has glucose, phosphorus, and carbohydrates in adequate measure so it is good for diabetics. Mountaineers carry coconuts with them to quench their thirst and hunger on high altitudes. Germs do not penetrate its shell so it remains edible for several months. Blessed with these sublime herbal and dietary properties, the coconut became a much sought after fruit for gifts, presents and also became an essential ingredient for many pleasant-to-eat dishes, including biscuits. The crop does not get damaged by rats or white-ants, reptiles or birds. Its timber is fibrous and strong so its stem is used to bridge rivulets, thus its farming is very economical and profitable.

It also has enviable chemical properties. Vaidyas (doctors) burn its outer shell to prepare tooth powder, cream for brushing the eye-brows, and for making some healing ointments. Its oil accelerates the healing of burns. To cure dehydration, it is advisable to mix a few drops of lemon juice in a cup full of coconut water and the patient is advised to sip the mixture for a sure cure. Its outer shell is used for making attractive handicrafts and bangles, toys and wall hangings. The burnt shell powder is extensively used in paint industry. Its husk is rich in strong fibres so it is used as a filler material for sofa set and cushions and car seats.

Spiritually speaking, this fruit represents and symbolises a deep rooted truth. In raw stage, it remains like any other being, quite undetachable with worldly belongings — the kernel remains inseparably attached to the shell just as every human being remains attached to worldly possessions; but when it dries up, the kernel detaches itself from the shell like a holy saint — totally detached from worldly attachments, and possessions so, when the shell is broken, pure and sweet kernel comes out for benefit of humanity like a holy saint.

"vajrādapi kathorāni, mrudinim kusmādapi, chetānsi ko hi vigyānumahtim."

Those who have succeeded in reaching the mind of man correctly, they can be impregnable as steel, and also tender like a flower. This is an apt description of coconut — hard externally, yet sweet and nourishing from within.

Thus, every inch of the coconut plants and fruit are a big boon to humanity. Hindus consider it a very auspicious

148

omen to receive or give this fruit. It is also called
SHREEPHAL because it denotes prosperity; Wondrous
dedication in the service of humanity without
discrimination!

* * *